Conversations In A Country Store

Reminiscing On Maryland's Eastern Shore

Hal Roth

Hal Roth

Nanticoke Books
Vienna, Maryland

Published by
Nanticoke Books
Vienna, Maryland 21869

First Edition

ISBN 0-9647694-0-9
Library of Congress Catalog Number 95-70484

Manufactured in the United States of America

To the memory of Glenn & Mary Wilson
who never made me feel like a "come here"

Contents

Introduction

In 1972 I purchased a small farm on a dirt road in Dorchester County on Maryland's Eastern Shore. In spite of my being a "come here," I was permitted to lay claim to the corner of an ancient and well-worn bench in a nearby country store and diligently began to study the art of hanging out. It was more than a store; it was a town meeting where most problems of the world were joined with a swift and practical resolution, and it was a stage where no performance was concluded without energetic applause. I loved the old people and their stories, and when, one by one, they began to disappear from their rostrums on the bench, the stool, the sacks of feed, I started to write down some of their tales. This book preserves a few of them.

There are accounts here of things that really happened, and there are folk tales and legends, stories that began as true narration but have been embellished over time by retelling. And there are, perhaps, a few fibs. You will discover no famous men and women on the following pages, and no events reported here will ever find their way onto the pages of history books. What you will find are glimpses into the life and lore of a small band of people whose lives evolved beside the rural roads and tidal rivers of an area still largely untouched by the frenzy of modern urban living. Here you will meet blacks and whites, men and women of modest origins and simple tastes, yet often possessed by an extraordinary capacity to survive. Here you will meet farmers, lumbermen, watermen, trappers, market hunters, bootleggers, and more. Most have already gone to their rest beneath the sandy soil that dealt them full measure of both hardship and kindness over long lives. I offer this book as a small token of my affection for each of them.

As with all folklife and folklore, readers may have heard variations of some anecdotes and raise questions about others. To them I shall reply, as one taleteller so earnestly stated his position, "It's the truth. He told me."

Acknowledgments

I am first of all indebted to the characters in these anecdotes and to those who spun the yarns – real people of this world and the true authors of this book.

A special thank you is owed to Glenn and Mary Wilson to whom the book is dedicated, to Howard "Jim" Willey, to Edmund "Ed" Wilson, and to James Spicer.

Jamie Dickerson has generously granted permission to share several excerpts from a taped interview she conducted with her grandfather, L. Leon Spicer.

My thanks to Carole Spicer for reading the manuscript and rescuing me from any number of embarrassing errors (those remaining are entirely my own), to Dr. Thomas Flowers for his gracious encouragement, and to Gregory Priebe for his valuable insights and recommendations.

The cover photograph was taken by George French and first appeared in *Countryman's Year* by Whittlesey House, McGraw-Hill Book Company, Inc.

Finally, I want to acknowledge the invaluable contributions of two ladies I love: Susan Hartman, for whom words are insufficient as thanks, and Sandy, who makes my every day a joy.

I wish it were possible to identify by name the source of each anecdote, but the majority of these yarns and reminiscences were told to me between ten and twenty years ago by individuals who are no longer alive or able to grant permission. The identity of several, I never did learn, and I would choose not to be explicit about others for the same reason I have changed the names of some characters: to avoid possible embarrassment. For consistency, then, I have not been specific about any of the sources.

The Country Store

"I just thought I'd do it."

I went in the store business in 1929, in March. I believe it was March 15. I'll tell you now: I heard the wind blow a time or two since then.

I just thought I'd do it. I helped to build this road out here; drove a pair of mules scooping dirt all up and down here. I tried to buy a place down below, but the man wouldn't sell it. Then I found out the old train station was for sale, so I bought that. I gave the man fifty dollars for the station and fifty dollars more to move it. It was just the station then, the waiting room with the benches all around and the ticket office. We moved it up here in the nighttime. You couldn't get on the road in the daytime or you had to have a permit. Damn! You couldn't of had more than two cars out there all day then. You likely had a Model T going in each direction, one in the morning and one in the afternoon. When a car come by, people stopped to look.

The station was vacant about a year before I bought it. There weren't enough business to keep it open. The line run from Ocean City to Claiborne, up there around Matapeake where the ferry went across the bay.

We put sills under her from one end to the other and put wheels under that; then we pulled her up here with a tractor in the dark. That's all there was at first: the old station. After a year or two we put two rooms on the back. That's when we moved up here. Then, after another year or two, we tore the roof and all the shingling off and went up with it; built the upstairs that time. Later on we added to each end.

1

We done good in them days. There weren't no more stores here. We had seven wholesalers come through every week. They'd come around and take the order and truck it in. We had all kinds of fresh meat then. We even sold work shoes what an old man would buy and bring up from Cambridge. We sold nails at five and six cents a pound. Stuff was cheap: eggs, a penny a piece; kerosene, four or five cents a gallon. Of course nobody used kerosene only in a light then. People would bring you eggs to pay their bill, or chickens. I had a little coop around back where I put 'em. They'd bring anything to swap. We were stocked up right good after about a year or two.

We used to buy huckleberries in season. We'd have thirty or forty cases setting out front every night. They'd come in from everywhere. We bought and sold 'em by the quart. I forget now what we paid for 'em and what we got, but we done all right. We packed the cases in the dark. You didn't know if you were eating a huckleberry or a fly. We would measure 'em out in quart baskets and put twenty-four baskets in a crate. Forty-two crates is the highest we ever had in one day. We had buyers come along and pick 'em up every night. They shipped 'em to the city; had a truck going to Baltimore every night. From here they'd go over to Hawkeye and pick up another fifty to eighty cases, then on to one place after the other, all around to all the stores.

I bought huckleberries from Monroe and from Glenny and others, and old man Jim. That was the old man's crop for the year. All he done was huckleberry. He carried ten-quart buckets, and he'd go everywhere. They was hanging in knots then, and you could fill a bucket in no time. I don't see none now. I don't know what's happened to 'em.

We used to have four gas pumps lined up: Gulf, Texaco, Holt Oil Company – Holt Oil Company was everywhere. It was Holt Oil, but it was Tydol gas. We had one more, but I don't remember what it was. Everybody come along and wanted to put in a tank. We sold a right smart lot of gas back then. We're cut back to one tank now, and I guess we'll have to give that up soon. The tanks got too old and they leak.

In the beginning we were open seven days a week, five or six in the morning and till ten or eleven at night. We'd always be up here till eleven on Saturday nights. You get up Sunday morning and the peanut hulls would be half-way up to your knees. I had an old battery radio setting on the shelf, and they'd come to listen to the radio on Saturday nights. Man, that bunch down in Tennessee – barn dances and all that stuff. It was pretty good.

We didn't have no electric then. Well, they had it, but you couldn't hook into it. The wire come over the middle of the field, but you couldn't hook into it; it was a high-tension line. We had two or three Delco generators and batteries. You'd have to charge 'em all the time. I never did have any new ones, just used. Somebody would get electric that would have one, and I'd buy it. I went to near about where the Bay Bridge is now for the first one – a hotel over there. They got electric and put this ad in the paper. Then I went way over in Delaware and got another one. They weren't nothing. Every time you needed it, something would tear up. When they did work, they was so dim you had to strike a match to find it. I don't remember exactly when we finally did get electric. Everybody had to sign up and guarantee the power company so much.

We had good customers and no trouble like you have now. I had bad trouble only one time: I think it was in 1933. It happened at nine o'clock at night. This little old coupe Buick – a one-seated rig – stopped out here, and they wanted gas. I put 'em in some gas, and then they wanted a quart of oil. While I poured the oil, one snuck around and come up behind me; hit me over the head with a pistol. It knocked me down, and I was running around on my hands and knees. I remember that, but I

3

don't remember them beating my head on the filler pipe that stuck up there. Mary come to the door, and one started after her. She ran to the telephone and cranked it up like she was talking to the sheriff. They left here then.

Next morning I couldn't even see. My head was swelled clean out even with my nose. They carried me over to the hospital in Salisbury and took x-rays. They said it wasn't busted through but was all cracked like a window, and I was all cut up from the hammer on that pistol and the filler pipe. They sent me home then, and I had to go to my doctor that night. He shaved my head and sewed me up.

They never did catch 'em. We had no near a sheriff there ever was in them days. He didn't even try to catch nobody. The only time you'd see him was if he thought there was a dinner somewhere. Some ones around here knew who it was. Come to find out they had a still down there in Ralph's old house, that one what was up there in the woods. And they had another house rented, and they had a still in there too. I was plowing over there one day, and it come up a thunderstorm. I wanted to get out of it. I didn't know somebody was renting the house, and I opened that door. Good God! In the front room there was barrels of mash setting everywhere. I wasn't long getting away from there, storm or no.

They lost their pistol out here and a hat; so we give that to the sheriff. After a time, when he didn't do nothing about it, I told him I wanted that old pistol back. That sheriff! We finally did get a pistol out of him, but it wasn't the one they lost out here, and we had a time getting that. Mary went up and down on him till he put one out. He was the worst sheriff we ever had.

Sixty years is a long time to stay with something. I don't mind it now, slow as business is, but if we had as much trade as we used to have, I don't think I'd want it. So what do you do? Unless you're sick, you hang in there. They have a sign over to the mill where we get our flour.

It says when you get to the end of your rope, you tie a knot and hang on. We're hanging on.

⁊⬤

My grandfather had a country store one time, and people would go there nights and Sundays and set around. He had an old pot-bellied stove in there with some wood into it. They'd set there and chew tobacco and spit on the side of that stove and tell funny stories. They could tell you something. Nothing in the world you couldn't hear in there.

Old man was talking one time: He said the North Star never moves. "Right where it's at," he says, "it stays there all the time."

Other man says, "It ain't so." Said, "My wife and I watched it in a knothole in the kitchen, and in forty years it moved a inch."

⁊⬤

Old Sam Jones had a store down to Church Creek, and that was the dirtiest thing I ever seen in my life. It was wood frame, two story, and I know it was a hundred, two hundred years old, and never had no paint on it since the day it was built. You couldn't see through the windows no more than you could see through the boards on the walls. It was a real place, yes sir, a real place! The old building leaned way out there and would of fell down, but he went out in the woods one day and cut some poles – big around as a stovepipe – and he propped 'em up there – four of 'em I think it was – all down the side to keep it from falling over.

Out front he had other poles planted – locust posts – and he put pipes across and wired 'em up there. He hung all his goods on them, the whole length of the building. He'd hang boots out there – only one to the pair – coats and dresses; all kinds of clothes: new clothes and old clothes.

5

And he had shoes piled up on tables, one to each pair just like the boots. He kept the other one back so nobody didn't steal 'em both. If you did want a pair, he never could find 'em both. It was a dirt road through Church Creek then, and everything out there would be all covered with dust. And if it rained, well, it would stay through the rain too. He'd hang beef out there all year 'round, right next to the clothes. In the summertime you couldn't see it for flies, big, green-headed flies, and the sun shining hot on it. People drove from all over Hell to see that place.

The floor inside went up and down like a roller coaster. Whenever I was in there, I never did see no boards on that floor, nothing but dirt; but I think there was boards under there somewhere. Sometimes he'd run a broom over it. He had a great pile of trash in one corner there, right where he pushed it. He never did shovel none out as I know. You couldn't see where you was walking. He had a little, teeny old light bulb stuck way up there for all it was worth. It didn't even cast a shadow. First thing you know, you'd be in a hole, and the rats running up the walls.

He sold everything in there from baby chickens to sewing machines. He had great lines of sewing machines upstairs, them old treadle machines.

I went in one day – I bought a little horse down below there in Crapo, and I went to fetch her. The wind was northeast and having a rain that day. It was chilly and cold. She looked all right – the little horse – so I bought her for thirty-five dollars and loaded her up. Coming up to Church Creek – that darn fool – she done everything she was big enough to do. She laid down flat on her back, feet sticking straight up in the air. I said, "Well, I guess now she's cold." So when I got there to Sam's, I stopped to get some burlap. I got about fifteen-cent worth and had all I could tote out of there. I wrapped that little horse all up in it. But what I started to tell you: when I went in there, it was a stack of jumpers laying with some cheese on the table.

6

While I was waiting for old Sam, some man come in with a calf he had just skinn't, and he throwed it right on top of that bunch of jumpers and overalls and stuff, no paper or nothing under it, and all that blood and everything. And a bunch of rats went running each-a-way. Five or six went up the side of the wall and through holes to the upstairs. I said, "My God, look at them rats go there!"

Sam said, "Oh, don't worry none about them. You're just strange. They don't know you."

Somebody left him a crab pot one time. He put it in the store that night with some cheese into it and caught some seventy rats. That's what they always told anyway.

He'd have a write-up in the paper every week: "Sam Jones' Best," and a mess of stuff all rhymed out. He used to advertise his candy for a quarter a box, a quarter for a pound box of candy. He'd go up to the city and buy it after these people had it go stale. I'll tell you one thing: he was right.

I can see old Sam now. He used to wear a little slouch hat with the brim pulled down. His hair was white, and he had a mustache. He wore glasses, old wire-rimmed glasses, and he wore 'em out on his nose.

Sam was a great church man, you know, and he wrote religious books and all that. He had 'em printed up and set out with a sign there in the store: "Books wrote by Sam Jones." He sold 'em for twenty-five cents or ten cents. Them books was full of stuff he wrote at two o'clock in the morning, or five o'clock, or whenever he took a notion. *A Book To Lead a Better Life*, stuff like that. Anything he thought of, he'd write it down.

Arthur Godfrey got him to New York one time before he died. He had him on television. Now that was comical. Old Sam had his jug of water right there with him. He showed it right on television. He went to Mardela and filled some jugs with spring water and took it with him. He wasn't gonna drink that New York water. He took a sack of oranges too. They say he threw them peels under his hotel bed. I know they was happy to see him come. Godfrey had come down here and went over to the store. He said it was the worst-kept store in the United States, which it was.

He had a nice house up the street. His wife died years before he did, and they said he never moved nothing. Everything was setting in that house just like it was when she died. He never dusted or nothing, just leave it setting right there. They tore the house down too, the house and the store both, years ago. There's nothing left of neither one.

ta.

I hauled help down to Golden Hill one time. They had a big track of timber down there. I used to carry 'em down there on Monday morning to the mill. I'd leave four, five o'clock in the morning. They gave me a dollar to pick 'em up on the weekend and carry 'em back on Monday. There was six or seven head I carried. I had a '27 Chevrolet at that time, a four-cylinder.

One day we were coming home, and Don Bowens said, "By God, let's stop by Captain Sam's and get a piece of cheese." He had all kinds of that. If you could eat it, he had it. Some of it could walk right out the store on its own. And cats would be laying right up there on that cheese block, all in there everywhere. He had plenty of cats around, always, and rats. The rats used to play with the cats, I guess. They sure didn't bother each other none.

So Don says to Sam, "Better give me two, three pound of that cheese, and how about giving me a couple of them pies." They was great big pies for a quarter or whatever it was. He'd just got his allowance. He didn't make but ten or fifteen dollars a week. So Don got all his groceries and loaded them up.

Now Don was an eating man, but everybody knows that. It's where the name Don Bowens' Bun come from. You know them old sticky buns used to be called Don Bowens' Buns. He could eat four or five of them anytime, and them as big as hubcaps.

So Don's setting on the front seat with me, and we're heading home. "By God," he says, "Sam Jones keeps good food." He broke off a great hunk of that cheese and ate it. By and by he bites down on one of them pies. When he got that one swallowed, he went for another one, went right on eating. "Damn!" he says after a bit. "That's the toughest pie I ever eat in my life." All of a sudden he looks down there and pulls the plate off what was left. "Goddamn!" he says. "I done ate the plate." You could see his teeth marks on the edge of what was left.

ﻭ

Old Charlie would open his store in the morning and put some change out. Then he'd go down to the river. He'd drink whiskey and tell lies all day down there, and people would just help theirselves and make change. He made a living and never worked a bit at it, and nobody never hurt him none as I know of.

ﻭ

He was a tight man kept store over there to Walnut Landing. He had a big store right down there on the wharf. When he'd go to weigh out coffee, they say, he'd take and bite a coffee bean in two to make the weight.

■

Birth

"She was the old granny momma."

My father used to say it was snowing a living gale when I was born. Snow was about boot-top deep, and the wind blowing a hurricane. He had to go get an old colored woman. You didn't go to no hospital, and you had no doctors. You go find a doctor in them days, and you'd be half growed before he showed up. Mandy Blake, an old colored lady down in Kraft Neck, would come up and take care of the baby. She was the old granny momma. I was born at six o'clock in the morning, so he had to go down while it was still dark and got her up. He said it was a perfect blizzard going on.

I had two sisters and two brothers, and we were all born right there in that bedroom, and old Mandy Blake taking care of us. That was all the help you had.

&

I always remember when my sister was born. They went and got the granny woman, Miss Lizzy. She come in the house with this basket over her arm.

After a while I heard a baby crying. I said, "What was that?"

My poppa told me, "Miss Lizzy brought you a sister."

Momma said, "Miss Lizzy brought you a baby sister in her basket."

I said, "Gosh! I didn't see no baby in that basket when she come in." I thought it was the funniest thing I ever heard, bringing a baby in a basket; but you know, it was a long time before I knowed any different.

All them granny women – every one I ever knowed – was colored. I never knowed even one to be white.

·

We saved our pennies for Billy's coming into this world. Doctor Coolman was our doctor. He got twenty-five dollars to deliver a baby, but we had to pay him thirty because he stayed all night with me. I was in a convulsion. The doctor begged me to go to the hospital, but I wouldn't go, and I come near dying. He said ninety-nine out of a hundred don't come out of it.

·

They carried my wife to Cambridge when my first boy was born. He weighed eleven pounds, and they had to cut her to get the baby out. She went three or four days and started up with a fever. By the fifth day she was really in bad shape. One of the nurses found they left a pad into her, and that got an infection set in. They put pads in to stop the blood, and they left one in there. She like to died. It was a long time before she got back on her feet.

·

When my mother was nursing, she said lots of mothers used to bite off the baby's fingernails so the baby wouldn't grow up to be a thief. And they used to carry the baby right upstairs when it was born and then bring it back down. I don't know why that was.

■

Education

"I had ice cream and cake one time."

My mother took me to school when I was six years old.
The teacher was named Marie, Marie Tubman, a very good
teacher. We never had a better one, but she was strict as all
outdoors, and she would knock the fire out of you if you
didn't do what you was supposed to. You could bet on that.
And my mother said, "Marie, I've brought Leon to school.
I want you to make him behave himself and teach him
everything you can; and if he misbehaves himself, switch
him and send me a note, and he'll get another one when
he gets home." That wasn't just talk; that was the truth –
the nitty-gritty of the whole thing, and she would put it
on you if you didn't do what she told you. The old saying
is "by the tune of the hickory switch." We were taught by
the tune of the willow switch. There was a big willow in
the yard, and when we did something we were not supposed to do, we had to go get a switch from the willow tree.

We had shortcuts to school. The roads were bad, and
sometimes the paths through the woods were better to
walk than the county roads. And sometimes the weather
was so terribly cold. When we went to school over in
Meekins Neck – over to Hickory Point – that was the first
woodland you hit where you go up that little hill going
across the marsh. From home to there was one of the
coldest places there was. When the wind was blowing
northwest or northeast, it really give you a fit. The old
people who lived up there on Hickory Point – the name was
Summons – were very, very, very poor people; but they were
nice people, and many and many a time she met us boys

12

out there to the road and made us come in the house and get warm. And many a time I walked facing the wind over there and crying from the cold. The old lady always had hot bread and butter, or potato bread, or a baked sweet potato for us. We thought a mess of the old lady. Poor soul, she had it hard.

When we got home from school, there were certain things we had to do unless we were sick: getting in the firewood at night; help feed the stock; gather eggs – dozens of chores. We'd come home and put on our work clothes and do the chores. We not only had to do chores in the evening, but we had to get up early enough in the morning to do a lot of chores before we went to school. And most children had to walk two or three miles to and from school. It took three-quarters of an hour each way most of the time.

When I was six years old, my father said to me, "Son, you're six years old tomorrow; you're going to milk the cow." So that was all there was to it. I can still remember the name of the old cow and what she looked like: Her name was Jane, and she was red with a little bit of white places on her. She had a real sway-back, but she milked easy. She had nice tits you could hold onto. I was proud of myself when I got that cow milked. I thought I was really something.

ᘐᐧ

I only got a paddling once. I and another fellow went to the toilet way down near about to the branch – an outside toilet. I had to go out. He was already down there, and he smoked. I don't know now if it was the principal or who it was come down there and caught us. I wasn't smoking at the time, but I was helping him strike matches. And boy, when we got back in the room, the teacher took a ruler and smacked your hands; she stung the devil out of you. That's the only time I ever got a paddling.

13

They want you to get your own switch in them days. If they were gonna beat you, you had to cut your own switch. What the boys would do was notch all around the switch, so the first time they hit you it would break in three or four pieces. They cut in there so you couldn't see it, you know, just with the blade.

My brother and me had about three miles to walk back and forth every day when I first started to school. There were some colored kids would walk with us. Course they wasn't in there with us; they had their school to theirself then. I think we had two grades to a room.

When we moved up to Mardela, I was the janitor in our schoolroom. I took care of the pot-bellied stove. We lived right across from the school; I could see right over there. I remember one time my brother and myself both had the measles. We were laying in there and had to do something. We had a mirror and throwed the sun over in the school with that mirror. Damn! We caught the devil for that.

In Vienna I rode a horse, or I rode with the Mulligan girls. They would come with the buggy, and they wanted me to ride with 'em. But most of the time I rode the horse and went to Johnny Webb. He had a stable there, and I put my horse right in his barn. Alan Webb had a store, and behind that he had an old shed for his customers to tie their horses in. That's what the Mulligan girls done. They tied their buggy in one of them stalls and left the horse to the buggy. It stood there from nine to four. That's how long school was. They had everything in that school, high school too. I quit in the seventh grade and went working on the farm.

When I started in school, there was just one room and one teacher. I had all twelve grades or whatever it was in that room. Lulla Bounds was the teacher, and her sister Hester was the substitute. They were both sickly all the time.

ია

The teacher over there to Walnut Landing – Nannie was her name. Man, she was mean.

Some fellow from up around Hurlock was running her. The man had a '24 Chevrolet, and he would come down all the time. He made an excuse that he cut a lot of cordwood down there.

It snowed one day. Man! It was two feet deep, and Nannie had sent all the children home 'cause of the snow. We come through there – you couldn't hardly get nowhere – and there was the old man's car setting off a little ways, and Nannie's horse and buggy tied up there. We crept up to the school and rapped on the door, I and my brother and Lester.

Nannie got mad at something, they say, and burned that school down. It did burn; I remember that.

ია

There weren't no school busses for a long time. You either walked or rode a horse, or some had a horse and buggy. Or somebody would drive a car and pick you up sometimes. I done that when I was starting out. I had quit school by that time. Emil Frase had a Model T that I drove for two years. I had three head I started with from up in Indiantown, and later on, when I got near Vienna, I had two or three more get in. We'd drive through the mud with that Model T; drive 'em to school. Now it was right.

ია

I never got no education. There was a school down on the edge of the woods about a mile from where I was raised,

15

right across from Carson's lane. They hollowed out a place there, about a half acre, and built a one-room school.

The last day of school they would make ice cream. They'd go up to Ned Willey's and get a piece of ice and make ice cream. I had ice cream and cake one time. I went to school for one full year. After that I went to school for two months or a half more every year. I did that until I was eleven years old, and then my father said, "Son, you're too big to go to school. I'm going to take you in the marsh with me. You can pole the boat and bring the traps and wait on me."

My sister went to school; she went to high school. I wanted to go to school too. I cried because I couldn't go to school. I used to study her books. I'd sit by the old coal oil light and go over what she had that day. I'd keep up with her. I done that four or five years, and that's what education I got.

I read an article in a magazine when I was about fifteen or sixteen years old. The man was talking about getting energy out of the sun and people flying through the air. I thought that was the craziest thing I ever heard. I thought the man was losing his mind, and I lived to see it all come true.

૨⚫

Old people like myself never got much education. When I was coming up, nobody had no education; thought education was a nuisance, a waste of time. My father went to school four days. He didn't get much education in four days. He started Monday and quit Thursday night. He could write his name just like somebody drawing a picture. He didn't know what it was, but he could write it. He didn't know if it was A, B, C, or what. His older brother had a right good education; he went to the fifth grade. He could read and write fairly good. But my father didn't like it when he started out, so he went four days and quit.

16

I quit school in the seventh grade. No, I think I got to the eighth. I don't think I passed it. I might of passed it. Doubt it.

We got most of our education from our parents. They taught us how to work. My father said many times, "I hope you don't have to do this kind of work. I hope you never have to come to it, but if you do, I want you prepared to do it and do it right." And that was it. We were taught to obey our parents, do the things we were supposed to do, and learn everything that was possible to learn from experience. We were not given much preparation as far as education was concerned. In those days a boy could go to school until he was eighteen or nineteen years old, but that was only part of the year. He'd go in the wintertime to take some of the books, the studies that he wasn't doing so good in, like mathematics. We were taught handwriting. We had copybooks, and there was a certain period in the day that was set aside for the use of those copybooks, and we were marked according to neatness and handwriting. We were taught everything that pertained to making an honest living. It was stressed very, very strong to always be honest and truthful.

Things were just so very different than they are now. There were no telephones or radio or electric lights, just the old coal oil lights. We had to get our lessons nights, around the table, around the old coal oil lights. The poorest families now have conveniences beyond what the rich had when I was a boy.

We always had homework. If we went to school and didn't have our homework done   unless you had a note from your parents saying there was a good reason you didn't have it done – why, you stayed in recess. You were

17

allowed to eat your lunch, but all the recess time you stayed in there and did the homework you were supposed to have done the night before.

≈

We didn't have no fire in school one time, and it was cold. Mattie McCready was our teacher, and everybody told her they was cold. One boy put up a window and crawled out, and he helped to catch the others. Everybody went home but the teacher. We left her. I don't remember what she said, but we went on just the same. It was easier getting out the window. If you go by the door you had to go by the principal.

■

Courtship & Marriage

"If it fits, then we'll get married."

Once in a while in the wintertime, somebody would have a square-dance. They'd get an old store or a house somewhere and get someone with a fiddle or accordion. The first time I ever saw my wife – they had an old store down below Cokeland, and they'd have square-dances in there once in a while. I couldn't dance – I had two left feet – but I'd go and look at them.

Two couples came down from Cambridge once, and they danced around for a while. I saw this girl a couple of times, there and up at Secretary. They had a square-dance up there too. I didn't know who she was or what her name was, but she was a good dancer.

Later on I was riding around Cambridge one Sunday night. I had this old car, and I parked it and was walking down the street. This girl came walking along by herself, and I said, "Where are you off to?" She said a few words and started walking off down the street. I followed after her and tried to start a conversation with her. I said, "You want to ride around town?" So she got in the car, and we went downtown.

After a while she said, "Well, I've got to go home," so I carried her home.

About a month after that I was going to the movies. They had an old opera house there. I was standing there, and she came walking along. I said, "You going to the movies?"

She said, "Yeah."

I said, "Let's go together."

"All right," she said.

19

I got two tickets, and we went in and saw the movie. It was only silent movies in them days, you know. We come out and got in that old car and rode around for a while. That kind of started things up, and I got to dating her a little bit.

After a while we went to the movies one night. It was a little over a year then, kind of steady off and on. After we saw the movie and got in the car, she said, "You know one thing: I want to get married."

I said, "You do?"

She said, "Yeah. I got a license in my pocketbook right now." She was nineteen, and I was twenty-eight, and I didn't think she wanted to marry a man twenty-eight years old.

I said, "Well, we'll get married then, I guess," and we got married.

⅋

You went down to the island one time to court a girl, you'd come out, and your horse had its tail bobbed and its mane cut off. Them boys down there used to be bad about that.

⅋

Some boy on the island took Willie's girl away from him one time, and he was upset. Captain told him, "Look here; I want you to go with me tomorrow night. We're going down there and get her back."

So they went down to the girl's house. She only had a walk-path from the road to the house. They could see the boy setting in there. In them days when you went courting, one set on one side of the room, and one set on the other side. They were setting there and talking.

Willie said, "What are we gonna do?"

Captain said, "The thing to do is scare the hell out of him so he don't come back no more."

Willie said, "How we gonna scare him?"

Captain said, "I'll tell you what: What will probably

scare him more than anything: when you see him in the doorway, we'll pull all our clothes off and jump out in the path at him." He said, "That ought to do it."

So they looked, and they waited, and after a while here the boy comes. Captain said, "My God, here he comes; get your clothes off. Just as soon as Willie had his clothes off, Captain grabbed 'em and throwed 'em down the well. Willie was on the lower end of the island, and he lived on the upper end, and he had to walk all the way home naked as a jaybird.

๛

I don't remember exactly where I met Mary, but I made a date with her finally. I wasn't going with her too long at that time, and we had a Halloween. My brother had just died that year – 1926 – and I was going some with her then.

You always had a big time in Cambridge on Halloween night. They closed Race Street, and everybody got all dolled up and go out there and dance from one end of Race Street to the other.

I had a Ford coupe then, a Model T. It was a touring car and had side curtains. I thought they'll liable to break the windows out of my coupe, so I used my pop's car that night.

We walked up town; I don't know how long. After a while I said, "Let's go back to the car." We walked down there and opened the door and got in. They had a dummy door on the driver's side. They didn't have no door you could open and shut; it was just the print of a door there. Unless you crawled in the window, you had to get in the passenger side and slide over.

So I got in, and she got in, and the minute I set down, some man said, "You son-of-a-bitch!" He grabbed right at the edge of the curtain and ripped it back. He come around that curtain and just did get the edge of my face. He said, "You got my wife!"

He was from Elliotts Island, I come to find out, and his wife was coming down there, and some man from Cambridge was courting her. I told him, "I ought to have you locked up. You tore my face up, tore my side curtain up."

He said, "Man, I'm sorry. I followed you all the way from Herbert Hearn's store. I was back in there and seen you come by, and she looked just like my wife, and you looked like the man with her." Oh, he begged, and he done everything. He had the children at home and got somebody to tend 'em, and he come on to Cambridge to see where she was. He knew she was running somebody, or somebody was running her.

Mary said, "Lock him up."

I said, "I can't have the man locked up, him in such a pickle." But you know: if he'd had a gun, he'd shot us right there. I said, "The hell with this place on Halloween. I bet I don't go here again."

ba

My uncle took a long time before he ever got married. He saw an advertisement: some woman wanted a husband. I don't know where she lived now – Chicago or some place way off somewhere. He got writing to her, and she decided she'd come here to see him. She wrote a letter – it tickled me. She said, "When I get off at the station, how will I know who you are from anybody else?"

He wrote back and told her, "I'll be there with a feather in my hat."

I had an old Model T Ford then, and I carried him down to the station to bring her up. Wasn't nobody there but him and her, but he had a feather in his hat anyway. She was city, you know. She expected a hundred people to be there, and she wouldn't know one from the other.

It wasn't too long, two or three weeks or a month, and they got married.

ba

Old man Carl advertised for a wife, and she came. He

was German. He met her at the station, and they went on home. He said, "We'll try it now and see how it fits. If it fits, then we'll get married."

I guess it must of fitted all right, 'cause they soon enough got married.

❧

It used to be a disgrace to be an old maid. I want to tell you right now that I think it's an honor and a pleasure. You can go when you want to go and come back when you want to come back, and you don't have to wait on no man in between.

■

23

Some Folks & Some Tales

"He was a terrible eating man."

There was a man named Peters lived in an old farmhouse, a great old farmhouse down there, just before you go down the other road, right there on that little hill. A farmhouse and a barn used to stand there, I know. Well, this man – I guess it was the Civil War – they used to pay somebody to go in your place if you didn't want to go and fight. This man Peters – I guess he didn't have no money – he went back there to hide from the government. There was some great old trees in that swamp – there's still some in there – and he crawled in one of them hollow trees and stayed there. His mother would bring him something to eat, and they always called it Peters Swamp after that. I guess when the war was over, he come out. I wouldn't of stayed in there with all them snakes if they'd been a whole army after me.

❧

There used to be an old house over to the edge of that road. It was rented out to a bunch when we moved down here, but they wasn't paying nothing, and they had got to bootlegging in there. They had lived in it so long I couldn't get 'em out. After the man got him for bootlegging, I said, "George, it's enough now; I want you out of there." They made me mad.

He said, "I ain't got no place to go."

I said, "Well, you'll go someplace, 'cause I'm gonna tear it down." I said, "I'm coming down here and tear the damn roof off. You'll be setting out, even if you're in." I went down and got up on the ladder and started on the shingles.

24

After about an hour, a wagon come with a pair of horses. They backed up there and moved somewhere.

That old house had huge sills in it, and she was all mortise and tenon. I used the old sills on the bridge across the ditch. That frame was just as solid as it could be, and it had big old dormers out in front. It was the worst thing I ever done: to tear that down.

 za

An old man lived in a swamp down below here, more than a mile back in there. He had a cart, and when he come to the store, he stood between the shaves and pulled it hisself. It was made for a mule, but he pulled it hisself. He'd buy his flour and things and take it back in there. They called it Bonnie Clabber where he lived in that swamp. His name was Jake Willey, and he raised a big family back there till they was growed and moved out. They lived off the land just like all of us done.

za

Lev was born and raised in that house and never left there. He was born in that house, and he died in that house. There's not many can say that anymore. He never worked a regular job in his life. He trapped and hunted and messed around the woods. Back in the thirties and the forties he mostly worked on old trucks and ground plow points and stuff like that. He had a lot of work then. Some days he wouldn't hardly charge you anything. Other days he'd laugh, "Ha! I put it on you today," and charge twenty what it ought to be. He was a hot old cat.

za

Captain Elmer was a old bachelor lived by hisself. They done all kinds of stuff with him. He would go to sleep up in the store, and they would untie his shoes and tie 'em together. Whenever he got up then, he'd fall out on the floor.

He'd want to whip the whole crowd in there.

Lev was always catching coons, nice fat coons, and he would cut 'em up and cook 'em. Captain Elmer would say, "Humph! I wouldn't eat no goddamn coons for nothing."

One night Lev says, "Ha! Ha! I'll get him." He took all the meat off some coons and made coonburgers, fixed 'em all up. In a little while, here come Captain Elmer up the road. Lev says, "Captain Elmer, come on in here and have supper with me. I've got some fine burgers made up."

Captain Elmer comes on in and sets down, and he eats one. "Goddamn, Lev, them things is good. I think I'll have another." He eat four or five of 'em till it was finished. When he left, he was walking up to Crossroads Store.

Lev called Captain Powell on the telephone up in the store. He said, "Captain Powell, Captain Elmer done eat 'em, and he loved 'em."

So he got up to the store, and a bunch got around and said, "Captain Elmer, we hear tell you tried to eat every coonburger Lev had down there tonight."

That settled it. He never eat down to Lev's again for the rest of his life, and he'd hardly speak to Lev again after that.

ẽ

Before Levin died – it was on a Saturday night when the wind blew – he called me. He said, "I want your opinion. I'm getting a tombstone made up. I'm gonna give 'em something to talk about. I'm gonna put a bust of Smokey the Bear on my tombstone."

I said, "Lev, I sure don't want to see nothing happen to you, but I hope I see it."

He died before he done that, but the boys had one made up, and they put Smokey the Bear on there big as life.

ẽ

Some of them old gentlemen lived down below here – they were peculiar. They were just sot in their ways. If they told you the leaves was white, and you knew damn well they was green, I would just say, "Yes sir, that's what it is."

≈

Old man Tom Harnage went down the road one day and come to old Ned's place. He stopped there and said, "Captain Ned, I just seen a man up there to town. I ain't seen him in twenty years."

Ned says, "Hell Tom, that ain't nothing. One went by here a while ago, and I never seen him before in my life."

Heh! Heh! The blamed fool.

≈

Cecil was always up to something when I was a boy. He was bigger than I was. John Beard – a man lived down there – done something to Cecil, and Cecil didn't like him. There was a pathway running around the orchard there by John's. Cecil said, "I'm gonna fix him. You go with me."

He went down there and made a snare. He bent a big old bush down – oh, great big as my arm – and he made a snare. He said, "If John comes around tonight, around this turn, he's gonna put his head in there, and I'm gonna pull him up. I'll have him here tomorrow morning."

I said, "You'll kill him."

He said, "I don't care if I do."

I said, "Now you don't want to kill the man." He had that thing all fixed up. I talked and talked to him, and I talked him out of it.

≈

Ezra had a boy, and he weren't too sporty. Like myself, he didn't have all the brains he needed. There come an old goose around to the pine woods, and she made a nest and laid her eggs. But something happened, and she left her nest after a week or two. "Ezra," I said, "a snake must of crossed her path, and she left her eggs."

The boy looked at them eggs and said, "Well, I'll set on her eggs, and I'll finish hatching 'em for her."

He set on them eggs for a long time, and anytime anybody come by on the road, well, he'd run on the road and sizz at 'em.

ॐ

Don Bouens had seven or eight head of children over there. He'd come home with four or five dollar at the end of the week, and he'd say, "Goddamn, I'm not making any headway, is I?" But he was getting filled up. He was a big man and a big eater. He tried to eat up everything he seen. He worked up to Wainwright's one time, and they put a big spread out there for dinner: chicken, 'taters, ham, anything you could mention. Don ate so much he couldn't walk back to the field. They had a sled out there they pulled around the field, and they got that. They hitched up a mule and hauled him back out there. He was a terrible eating man.

ॐ

We used to have a boy would help us here. We called him Dink. He was raised by Sam Cephas and lived across the branch. He never went nowhere; just stayed around here, Saturday nights and all.

One time the Bouens boys wanted to go to Cambridge, and Dink got a notion to go with 'em. Well, they got down there and went on Pine Street, and the boys kicked up an argument with another bunch. Now Dink wouldn't bother nobody, but they were his buddies, so he run right out of his coat to help 'em. Just about that time the Bouens boys flew off, and here come the cops and grabbed Dink and locked him up. I'll bet he hadn't been to Cambridge before in his life.

The next morning old Sam come over and said, "Dink is in jail." Well, we went down as soon as we got straightened around here. I think it was ten dollars bond to get him out.

But when we got down there, here's Gene Moore – him what run the ferry in Vienna – and he's in jail too. He said, "Get me out of here. They won't take my check."

What happened: Gene went over there with his friend Elwood the same night as Dink. Now old Gene liked to drink a little bit, and he was setting there on the street pavement waiting for Elwood. Elwood was courting down there somewhere. Here come the cops and said he was drunk, and they carried him off to jail. He had the money, but he only had his checkbook. Of course they wouldn't take a check. His bond was ten dollars too. I got 'em both out.

You could not go to trial then, and they'd just keep that bond. They never did go back and stand trial.

※

Old Cleve – I can see him now. He had an old mule and wagon with a set of shaves instead of a tongue. You backed that mule in there between those shaves and hooked 'em to the mule's collar. He'd load that wagon up with tomatoes and come four miles up the road to Baker's. He didn't like Baker, so he'd go past him another four miles up to Sewell's. He'd sell to Sewell and didn't get a penny more from him than Baker was paying.

※

John Good lived by hisself. He went home one night, John did, and sat on his old davenport playing the mouth harp. Now Cecil had gone in there before John got home and got underneath that old place. He was laying underneath there when John started playing his mouth harp. Once in a while – it was all open in there anyway – Cecil would reach out and tickle him around the ankles. John would look and cuss, and he'd play the mouth harp some more. Wouldn't be long before Cecil would be tickling him again, pulling on his ankle. Finally it got so bad that

29

John took off running. Cecil done all that funny stuff.

ε‌

Glenny and his Model A – now they were something. He'd jack her up and crank her with the hind wheel, with her in gear. It's a wonder he ain't been run over and killed and everything else. He would come home at lunch and change the engine in her. He done that several times. He only had two bolts to hold the drive shaft up there to the motor. The motor was just setting in there flopping around, but it hung up somehow. He'd come home, and it wasn't just right to suit him; he'd throw the engine out there on the woodpile. I mean I seen him do that. He'd pull one cylinder out, one of the pistons. She'd go, "shush, shush, shush, shush." It didn't have no power, but he could get around with it.

They sent him over to Salisbury for something. He got as far as Turpin Branch, and there he was, working on that car. Lloyd Lankford come by, and he said, "Glenny, can I help you?"

"Nope," Glenny says. "She stop on her own 'cord, and she gonna start on her own 'cord."

Lloyd went on to Salisbury, and when he come back, Glenny was still there. "Glenny, you sure you don't want me to help you?" he says.

"Nope," Glenny says. "I told you: she stop on her own 'cord, and she gonna start on her own 'cord." He ain't never got there yet.

ε‌

Now that man – I want to tell you – he was a character in this week. They outlawed him from driving a car for drunk driving, so he gets a tractor. Next thing – he's the only one I ever knowed – the police outlawed him from driving a tractor. He was always drunk. So then he got his-self an old mule, and he'd take the old mule over to Linkwood a-riding on the shoulder of the road. He'd get finished over there and climb back on that mule. That old mule knew just where to go. And back they'd come, him setting up there drinking a beer, and that old mule just walking right along on the shoulder. Everything he done was two backwards and one forward. His reverse was a lot better than his forward was.

ॐ

Them two families – the crowd that used to have my place and the ones next to 'em – my God, they were lawing all the time. They lost that place by lawing, all of it. They owned everything one time, all the way across to this field here. They surveyed just about every week or two trying to take each other's property, and they all lived there side by side. They just went on lawing and lawing and lawing. They just went on fighting till they all died out.

ॐ

People lived all over the woods once and on them islands in the marsh. The Grays lived in a great old house way out across that marsh. They had a road going out there – they called it a road, anyway – and a wood bridge. Most of the time you couldn't get over there for the water, and it was ruts so deep even the horse and buggy would get lost. Most of the time they just went up the bay in a boat. When it froze up, of course, they had to walk all the way across to Axies Island where the Elliotts Island Road come by. The kids had to walk all the way across there, and then all the way to Elliott to go to school. That's a long way. In the wintertime I don't know how they done it.

They moved to Elliott later on, and the old house fell down; maybe it burned – I forget now. It was a right smart graveyard out there. They say a man pushed it up to make a duck pond. When they lived on Elliott, people called them "Brothers of the Brush." They caught skeeters – one of

31

'em did – and sold 'em by the quart to somebody. There was an old road there through the pines to 'em. If you ever got started in there, you better try to keep going. The trees was so close they scraped the fenders. I come out with a boy one time – he throwed it right to the floorboard and bust through; and when he struck the road, she jumped and went right across. I said, "If somebody just come down this road, you're a dead duck and me both."

He said, "It's the only way you can get out." He had an old Plymouth.

ૐ

Ham said he was out fishing one day, and he run out of gas out there in the ship channel. He looked down the bay, and one of them big tankers was coming up right on him. He said to himself, "Ham honey, you got to do something or that ship's gonna run right over you. It's going to be your death right here." He said he looked all over that boat. Said he went forward in that pilot house, and there was a can of blackstrap molasses in there. He said he told himself, "Ham honey, this molasses is your last chance." He said he went back there and took the cap off that gas tank and poured the whole gallon in there. Said it only turned about three times, and it caught. He said, "I poured her ashore." He said, "I kept noticing the bow was raising and the stern lowering, and I couldn't figure out what it was. I turned around, and that son-of-a-gun was spitting out the purtiest little ginger snaps you ever seen." He said he had to shovel 'em overboard to keep her floating. He said, "I know I must of shoveled a million dollars overboard."

Ham caught a rockfish one time and said it was so big he had to scale it with a hoe. Said he took and shingled the house with them scales, hollowed the head out and made a chicken house with it, and he used the bones to build a picket fence.

ૐ

Everett and Lewis bought this great big old car one time. I'm almost thinking it was a Packard. They run her and run her and run her. It was a convertible.

Now there was a preacher in the neck had a string of churches clear down to the islands. He told Everett if he ever decided to sell that car, well, he'd really love to own it. By and by Everett decided to sell it to him. It wasn't too much money, but the preacher couldn't pay cash. He said, "I'll have to pay you installments." Everett said the only way they could collect their money was to go to church services on Sunday. He'd take up a collection, and that was where they'd get their payment, out of the collection plate.

The preacher never did drive, and the stipulation when they sold it to him was that they had to teach him. One day Everett and Lewis were teaching him how to drive, and he had his wife and little boy along. The reverend was at the wheel, and Lewis was up front showing him how to shift gears and all that. Everett was in the back seat with the reverend's wife and boy, and they were driving through the neck. They used to go down to a bald spot where salt had come in the field and it wouldn't grow nothing. There's a lot of 'em down there. They'd pull in there, and that's how they turned around. The reverend swung her a little short and had to back up. There was a pine thicket and a barbed wire fence in there. He put her in reverse. They said he had a foot on him – must of been size fourteen. Said he stomped down on that accelerator, and away she went; struck the pine bushes; reared up on her side and got hold of that fence. Everett said just about that time everything went black, and he thought he was choking. He thought they'd turned over in the marsh. Come to find out: when they were thrown around back there, the reverend's wife got her legs wrapped around Everett's neck, and there he was with his head under her dress.

෧

I had a sister was a tall girl. I'll tell you now: she was tall. A man needed a stepladder to kiss her.

She had a flat tire one day, and she waited alongside the road. These two men come along and wanted to know could they help her. She said, "Yep. I got a flat tire, and I got a spare in the trunk."

They lifted up the lid, and there's no jack in there. One man said, "Ma'am, you don't have a jack, and we don't have one either."

She said, "That's O.K. I'll lift it right up, and you put the tire on there," and she lifted it up. That's the God's truth. These two men hurried up and got that tire on, and they got in that pickup and left there.

When my father came to this country – I was the only one born here – he used to hook up her and the other two girls and plow the ground.

❧

Old Warden, that poor man, he couldn't put one foot in front of the other but he'd fall down, and he was always wanting to go ducking with me. I'd carry him in the marsh – it was a terrible place to walk in there. You miss one of them tussocks out there, and you was lost. I would say to him, "Warden, you miss one of these tussocks and you gonna get wet." My God! "Kerslup!" There he goes, just a swirl of water and mud.

❧

If they wanted to kill a beef way back in them years, they would swing it up a tree limb, and somebody up the tree would shoot it. Well, they had this beef swung up there, and the old man in the tree was cross-eyed. He got ready to shoot, and this fella on the ground said, "Wait now, do you shoot where you look?"

Old man in the tree said, "Yes sir, I sure do."

Man on the ground says, "Then you let me get away

34

from here, 'cause you're looking right at *me.* "

&

There was a man down here one time claimed to be bad. He strutted about and showed his pistol all the time. I heard him say, "I ain't scared of nobody. I got this pistol here, and I'm gonna come down this road when I want."

Some of the boys wanted to straighten him up a little, but they was worried about that pistol. So they made a plan.

Chuckie said to him one day, "We like to coon hunt, you know, but we're tired of toting our .22 rifle and shotgun. Can we borrow your pistol some night? It's easier to carry. We want to see if we can shoot 'em out with a pistol."

"Yeah Captain, she's just right. You take her."

But they didn't really want that pistol. They took her and pulled the firing pin out of her, and they give her back.

Now it come a moonlit night, a great old full moon down there on Steels Neck Road, and they laid for him in that ditch there. They put a lantern underneath a sheet and had it turned down. After a while, here he comes. When he got off there a little bit, they raised that sheet up, spread it all out, and took off after him. Now you talk about running; he left there. You could hear his feet half a mile down the road. They said they never had to worry about no pistol; he didn't even try to get to it. He run all the way through Kraft Neck, about eight miles. Said he run so hard it like to kill him. He never was no more good to work after that.

&

A fella lived up the road here one time, and he had a goat. He come home for dinner one day and kept hearing something upstairs. He thought there must be somebody in the house. Just then a shingle went by the window. He went and got his shotgun then. It was a two-story house, and right up there on the ridgepole was his old goat running up and down. He waited till it got out to the edge and let one go: "Payoww!" That old goat sailed right out there and flew. It never hurt him none. What it was: he drove his car up close to the porch, and the old goat went up on his car and up on the porch roof and on up.

ꝫ

One thing Mr. Haddaway could do: he would make ox whips. He would make the staffs and plait 'em, and then he'd put one in each hand and play "School Days." I've heard him do that. With one in each hand, boy, he would just crackle 'em to the tune of "School Days."

ꝫ

They used to have a brickyard down here, and my great uncle went and loaded his wagon up with bricks one time. It was raised up where you loaded, and he was afraid the horses couldn't hold back enough, so he put them out and rolled it off hisself. That wheel got away and busted the side of his head. The skin fell right off his face. He slapped it back, but that mark carried to the grave.

ꝫ

It was when the First World War was going on – they built ships up to Sharptown in them days. John had a little timber, and he cut some special oak for the shipyard. One day he was going up there with his timber cart – I think it was four mules he had to that cart – and I went along with him.

He chewed tobacco, and he was showing me how he could spit between his fingers. He was always carrying on with me anyway. He said, "I can spit between your fingers too; let me show you."

I said, "All right," and I held my fingers up there. Damn! He spit the whole gob right in my palm.

When we got near about to Sharptown – we done crossed

Plumb Creek – he said, "I know the man's got a watermelon patch back in there. Why don't you run in and get us one?" It was warm weather, and I thought a watermelon would taste good while we rode on that timber cart. It looked a long ways, but I took off. Damn! Wasn't a watermelon patch nowheres. He said, "Well, I guess the man must of moved it." But we carried that wood to the shipyard. They were working on a ship then.

I remember the last ship they built up there. I was going to school in Vienna then, and it pulled in there and layed up, I guess a week or so. It was a big four-master, and she was lost on her first trip out.

ð

Babe worked for Clay Webb one time. Clay sold fertilizer and all that stuff. Babe said that Charlie wanted some fertilizer one day. He told Clay to send Babe with some and lay out a bag, one here and one there, all around the field where he had some tomatoes. So Babe put 'em out there. Charlie come along and opened the first bag. He turned the top down a little, put it under his arm, and started throwing it around his tomatoes – a two hundred pound bag.

Babe stayed there and watched him a long time. Whenever he got back, Clay said, "Where the hell you been?"

Babe said, "I was watching this man pick up a two hundred pound fertilizer and throw it right out the bag."

Clay said, "Shit, that ain't nothing; he always done that."

ð

If you ever want a tough one, there was old man Chester. God! He was tough! He had a little patch over there where the hunting club is now. He had an old mule and a cart, but he said he didn't need it. He'd put a bushel on his back and tote it to the barn, dump it out, and come back for another.

Old George made whiskey right out to the end of that lane, and old man Chester would send some boys over there to get some in their bootleg. They was toting for him all the time. It never hurt him none.

The old man had cancer for years and years, and his water would give him trouble. I guess it was in his bladder. He'd take basket wire off the tomato basket – it all rusted and everything – and shove it up in there to open him up. Ed went down there one day, and he had it all hung up. He got it up there and couldn't get it out, and the old man was bleeding. He said to Ed, "Ed, I want you to get this thing out of here," and Ed pulled it out.

God sake! That old man been living today if he hadn't froze to death when his shack burned and left him outside. He was 95 or 96. It was cold and raining that night, and it froze up. The old man used to take coal oil and pour it right on top of the coals – one room and his bed right by the stove. He had to put out fires lots of times. That night nobody come by, and nobody knew about the fire till next morning. Leon stopped in there, and the place had burned down, and the old man layed there by the steps. He crawled out, and there he was naked, and it so cold. He must of tried to get up there to the coals to warm up. Some said he burned to death, but I went over, and he didn't have a burned place on him.

He scared the shit out of me one time. I felt like killing him. I went over there to carry him back in the woods to show me the boundary lines. He come out of that shack, and he said, "Wait a minute; let me carry my gun. Maybe I'll see a rabbit." I never seen him put any shells in it. I was walking behind him, ahead of him, and everywhere else, and looking right down the barrel of that damn thing half the morning. We came back, and he says, "I'd better take the shells out. She goes off once in a while." I like to fainted. Ed said it went off when he moved it in the corner one time and blowed a hole right through the roof. And we ain't never seen no rabbit, and he didn't know where the boundary line was a bit more than me. I had a great mind to kill him. I was so mad I would of fought a bear and give him the first bite.

❧

You can't let every little thing worry you or you'll never do nothing. Old Joe is the greatest about that. He won't eat nothing in cans or something like that.

He hauled stringbeans to the canning house one time, put 'em in granner bags and hauled 'em up there and dumped 'em out. They had this man scooping 'em up and throwing 'em in a vat. He was chewing tobacco, and he spit in 'em. Joe seen that, and right away he thinks every stringbean is bad.

Joe won't drink nothing out of a can or out of a bottle but what you can see through it. He won't drink none of them soft drinks anymore. He's always scared somebody got a cigarette butt or a mouse or something like that in it. Of all people to find a cigarette in one, it was him. He bought a ginger ale and hadn't opened it. He took it back and they give him another one. With some people, now, I imagine the company had been in trouble, but Joe didn't fool with it.

He won't eat a hot dog or a sandwich away from home, nothing at all like that. He went up the road with Bobby one morning to New Jersey. He was gone all day long and drank neither drink or ate neither piece of food up there or back, but he had some whiskey underneath the seat. He'll drink that, but he won't touch another thing. He's eighty-two and never eat neither sandwich in a store in his life as I know.

❧

Babe was driving his combine up the road one day, that old red International he had. Now you know how big a combine is. Just then, here come Cooper up the road in his car. There ain't neither another car in sight, and "Wham!"

Cooper run right up his ass end. Babe climbs down out that combine, and he says, "Cooper, what the hell you doing?"

Cooper says, "Damn Babe, I never seen you."

⁊⁊

Wasn't a man around as strong as Frank Cephas. They had mills all over the woods in them days, and they was always hauling 'em somewheres. They had a sawmill back here, and they come to move it. They had this great old steam boiler on the wagon. It wasn't nothing but ruts in that road, and it got rough. The old boiler started to rolling off the wagon. Now this was a great old steam boiler, and Frank went around there and grabbed it and held it right there till they got it strapped back. Any other four men would of tried that, and it would of rolled right over 'em.

Frank used to fire the boiler down to the canning house. He always had them red flannel drawers on, and all wrapped up in a greatcoat, and he'd be throwing that coal and wood in there.

Man said one day, "Frank, you're gonna smother to death."

Frank said, "It keep out the cold, and it keep out the heat."

He wore them red flannels winter and summer, and he had arthritis. His great old hands were always swelled up. Every time I seen him he smelled like liniment.

⁊⁊

When I was a youngster, twenty-dollar gold pieces was all the rage. Nelson was always trying to get twenty-dollar gold pieces, and he gathered 'em up everywhere he could get 'em. Anybody owed him, or any work he done, he'd get a twenty-dollar gold piece and put it in his bag. He had two bags full, and he kept 'em in the bedroom. I seen 'em many a time. I guess them two bags weighed fifty pounds apiece. They was big around and tall, and they closed with a string.

A few years later, you had to turn all your gold in. You couldn't keep no gold, and that broke his heart. I think it was almost three thousand dollars when he turned 'em in.

ﾞﾞ

When my uncle died, he had a little money in the bank and a little in the house. He had an old shed back behind the house where he kept his meat, and back in that shed he had a bunch of junk and some old timber chains in the corner. After he'd been dead about a year, they were trying to clean that stuff up. When they moved that chain, they found a Prince Albert Tobacco tin, one of them big, round ones. It had nine hundred and some dollars into it, five and ten-dollar bills stuffed in that old tobacco tin.

ﾞﾞ

Damn! Old Arrowhead! He takes that dead corner to your place right wide open. He'll meet somebody some day, and it won't be easy, just like it wasn't easy how he got his name.

You never heard that story? His brother and him was out in the field shooting arrows one day. They'd set the target up on these bales of straw, and he'd sit down behind it while his brother shot the arrow. Now you might think I'm going a little Robin Hood on this, but this is right. Well, he hid behind these bales of straw, and he thought it was taking his brother a long time to shoot, so he raised up to take a look. "Thwack!" That arrow struck him right square between the eyes. He had to get the hospital to take it out, and that's why they call him Arrowhead. I mean she went right in there. I guess it wasn't funny when it happened, but there's been some leg slapping over it since then.

ﾞﾞ

You see where this woman down in Cambridge lost three fingers cut off, and they find 'em in a can of sweet

41

potatoes way up the road. They didn't want it to get out, but somebody found them fingers in their can, and they traced it right back to Cambridge. I guess some judge will hear about that.

છ

They say something can turn your hair white just like that. Miss May – they say her hair turned white overnight. It was just as white as paper since I knew her, but she had enough on her to kill anybody. Ten or fifteen kids, and everywhere she went, they had a fire. Every house they ever lived into burned down.

છ

Nellie, of course, she did have her men. You talk about the 'taters of today; well damn, she was a 'tater of her time. She had a bunch of boys, and neither one of 'em had the same daddy. She was a character. If she had a man in there, she'd put the lantern on the gate post. If the lantern was hanging, you couldn't come in; you had to wait your turn. That one preacher down there – they was looking over his stuff when he died, and there was a check made out to Nellie: "Two dollars, for services rendered."

■

Country Living

"Them city folk don't do nothing to get dirty."

It's the funniest thing: you come in from outside and get warm quicker by a wood stove that you can by a oil stove. I don't know why that is, but you can. My word! That old kitchen stove of ours: you could bake in it and everything. When the boys would come home nights, we'd play some music there in the kitchen, and they'd bring oysters. They'd put them oysters in that oven and roast 'em, put 'em in a pan till their mouths would open. Course I don't like 'em.

᠊᠊

People lived off the land when I was a boy. You got huckleberries and muskrats and squirrels, and some had a spot where they could plant a little cabbage and beans and potatoes or something. Most didn't have no land what amounted to nothing. If they had a garden, they had to till it by hand. Weren't no mules or horses. They'd spade it up by hand and grow a few bunches of vegetables.

There was plenty of game – oh my lands – and plenty of forest. I don't mean bushes like now; I mean trees, big trees, a world of 'em. All kinds of things in them woods, everything under the sun you could think of. You could always take your gun or your traps and catch something to eat – no problem. A lot of people on the river fished and muskratted, sold the fur and eat the meats. You didn't have no employment. My father never had a day's salary in his life.

I would set rabbit gums with the first frost. Paw never

let me set the gums till the frost fell. He said the rabbits had wolves into 'em, and the frost killed the wolves. That was true; he was right about that. They were big old worms into the back of the rabbit, and the frost killed that. I never thought the wolves would hurt 'em, but Paw wouldn't eat none if the wolves was into 'em. I would catch anywhere three to four rabbits just about every morning in my gums, and we'd have rabbits from then on for dinner and supper. The gums were square boxes. I had seven or eight or nine. Wherever I found a rabbit track around the field, around the edge of the woods, I'd set a box there. I don't know why they got the name. Ever since I was a boy they called 'em gums. It was bad weather if I didn't catch two or three rabbits, and we'd eat 'em fried, stewed, and every other way.

❧

People believed in the old saying that idleness was the devil's workshop, and I agree with that right much. When a boy got to twelve or fourteen years old, they could replace a man working in the fields or in the woods, and I think that was much better than now when children are not allowed to work until they're pretty near grown. I think we would have a lot less trouble if they were allowed to work, something to tire them out, and they'd be ready to go to bed.

In those days nobody made any money, hardly, but there were awfully decent men that had families and all. A lot of them had big families, bigger families than there is nowadays. My father would tell them when it would come a long, cold, snowy spell or something, "Don't suffer. Come up here, and I'll do something for you." He used to butcher an awful lot of beefs and hogs and all, and have salt meat. Sometimes he'd give them some of that to help them through, and many times he'd give a credit to go to whichever store was closest to them, but they weren't supposed to come and ask for help until Saturday evening. In those days you'd work six days a week, and long days. Wasn't no hours to it. They'd get their oxen before the sun come up and work till after dark.

Winters were a lot rougher than they are nowadays. Everybody was taught to be prepared for winter. Men had a coop with chickens and ducks, and hogs in the pen, and a garden; and in the fall of the year they dug potatoes and pulled up the turnips and bunched together the cabbage.

❧

It was a job to keep food in the old days. One time we used to have the old milk trough – we called it a milk trough. It was a big trough of wood, well, maybe two feet wide and as long as you want, as much as you want to put in there. It had holes in the end. There was a screen over and a lid on it. Air would come in, and that was all you had. You set the food in there, and the air would draw across it. You'd use it mostly in summer. In the winter you just set food up where it didn't have no heat.

Some had a meat trough with salt in it to preserve the meat, to pickle it. We'd use a crock sometime to pickle it. We used to mostly salt the meat.

There weren't no refrigerators, but some had the old icebox. You'd put a block of ice in the icebox to keep things cool, but we didn't have that. In the wintertime you could go up to the millpond and cut ice. Some would cut it – Pop always told about that, but I didn't see it – and they would put it in a pit with sawdust on top, and that would keep it from melting. You could dig some out then when you want it. If you done that right, he said, it would last into the summer.

If you had a dug well, you would put stuff down the well. You know, I think that would keep better than it would on ice, just as long anyway. You had a rope to lower it down there. There were lots of dug wells then. When we were little kids, they were always saying, "Get away from that well; you'll fall in there." They'd have it boarded up around the top, or some would have it bricked up. If you had a running spring, you could dig that out and put a barrel in there. I had one over the branch. I went there one day to get a drink of water, and there was an old rabbit fell in and drowned.

Apples and turnips and stuff like that – you'd just bury them. You called it a kill. You'd scoop off a little dirt and put the stuff in there on pine shats – something under it. You just put the turnips in the dirt so they wouldn't freeze. The potatoes you'd keep like that too if you didn't have a cellar.

ૐ

Men usually did the milking, and the women bottled the milk and made the butter and cheese. When we had a lot of milk, we had a few regular customers. It was five cents a quart, or some would ask for a penny's worth. First thing: you would strain it and filter it to get the hair and dirt out. Then it was cooled before you put it in bottles. You dipped it out of the cooler can and into a funnel to fill the bottle, and then you put a paper cap on top. Your customers had to bring the bottle back, and you would sterilize it and fill it over and over again. That was raw milk, and heavy cream would form on top of the bottle.

ૐ

There was always plenty enough for several women to do around the house. Cooking and baking then was a lot different than it is today. It took a lot longer to do things, and you had to make everything yourself. One thing I liked to do was to make butter. Mom said she used to make butter in a wooden churn, but the one she had that I remember was a crock. It had a wooden stick through the lid with a churn on the bottom. You worked that up and down through the cream till the butter would get hard. But what I used was a

46

gallon jar with a crank on the top of the lid and paddles inside that would spin around. That was a lot faster, and later on they even had electric ones. I still have my old one.

And we made our own cottage cheese. You put your raw milk in a bowl or pan and let it set for a day or two until it formed a clabber. That you would tie up in a cloth bag and let all that juice drip out. Finally, you squeezed it and you had your cheese.

But I didn't finish telling you about the butter. After you took the butter out, you would work it with wooden paddles to get all the buttermilk out, and you would wash it. You had to let the butter set in some cold water and keep changing it till all the buttermilk was out. You salt it and put it in crocks then, or you could make it up in what we called prints. Then you put it in the ice box or down the well or whatever you had. Those old butter prints bring big money now in the antique stores. Some of them had pretty designs cut into them, and that's what people want today to set on the shelf. Every farm had its cow or two, and you were always busy making things from the milk.

≈

I was over to Kraft's one time, and the old man was having trouble with his well. He couldn't get no water. He was having to drive a new pump, and he didn't know where to put it. Old John Tjaden came up there. John cut a forked stick out of a peach tree and walked around there, and after a spell it commenced to bobbing up and down. He said, "Put your pump down here." Mr. Kraft done that, and it was good, sweet water he got. A piece out of an old peach tree, and you walk around till it gets to wiggle, and there's water there. Old John was German. He was the only one I ever seen use that.

≈

When I was a youngster, I used to get my forked stick

and go around and look for water. They couldn't find no water down in the neck. They drove three or four wells; had one seventy-five feet, one thirty feet, and everything else. The boss come to me one day and said, "Somebody told me you could find water."

I said, "Yeah, I can find it."

"Well," he said, "you come down and see if you can find some. We got to get that timber out." They used steam skidders, and they had to have water for steam.

I got my forked stick and walked all that swamp and 'round about, and I never got as much as a tremble. I got out close to the field, abut two hundred yards to the field, and my little stick started ticking over. I said, "Put your pump right down here." I said, "It's right on top of the ground. You won't have to go more than fourteen or fifteen feet." There wasn't much, but it was enough for the boiler. That was the only tremble I had over the whole swamp.

I always used peach. You get over a stream of water, and it'll tremble. You can feel it. I've done it many a time. You got to get the right size and the right fork, just so you could grasp it. You got to be particular about your fork: The biggest part wouldn't be as big as your little finger, and it comes down to the size of a lead pencil, about twenty inches long. You hold one fork in each hand, and when you hit water, you can feel it. The fork would want to dip a little, and you can feel it in your hands. I haven't done it – golly day – the last time I ever done that must have been in 1930 something. If you feel a little tremble, put your pump right down there, and you'll get some water.

&

You had nothing much to take baths in the old days, a little basin or something like that was all. Pop always said it was backwards: the farmer had nothing, and the city folk had the bathtubs.

"It's the farmers what need the bathtubs," he always

said. "Them city folk don't do nothing to get dirty."

ja.

Fred Fleetwood used to say everybody would eat their dinner in the house, and then they'd go out to the backhouse to do their business. Nowadays then, everybody wants to eat outdoors, and then they come in to do their business. It's all got turned around.

ja.

People today, with all their vacuum cleaners and steam cleaners, they don't know what it is to clean a rug. We used to do it with a wire beater. That's the only way we had to do it years ago. Sometimes it would take days to clean a rug – a big one. You done it two times a year: in the spring and in the fall. It would hang outside on a line, even the big carpets from the parlor, and you had to beat it with a wire beater. It was enough of a job just to get it hung out there on a line. We strung up a special wire. It was too heavy for the clothes line. Some used sticks, just an old, wood stick or a switch, but we had several wire beaters with wood handles on the end. You beat on that rug – dust just flying everywhere – till you saw stars, till you couldn't lift your arm no more. Then you'd beat on it some more after you took a rest or done some other work for a while. And you'd want to air it out, you know. You never could finish it in one day, not if it was a big one. Usually you took it in at night and hung it up again the next day. It took several head to get it done. You'd hang it up on the other side and beat on that side then. It was a job, I'll tell you that. Nobody liked to do it, but you had to get it clean, and that was the only way to do it.

ja.

It used to be that most farms had a poor family lived right on the place. If a farm was any size, like fifty or sixty acres, they had a tenant house out there somewheres, and there'd be a family lived there. The house was free, but they worked for it. Nearly everybody that had anything halfway or had any income had somebody helping around the farm and the house.

ء๑.

There wasn't much separation between the white and the colored if you lived in the country. Everybody worked together, and when you needed help, everybody pitched in. At wheat thrashings a lot of colored ones helped out. They did have separate tables. They didn't eat off the same table. The white ones eat to theirselves and the colored ones eat to theirselves. There was that much separation around here.

Most colored ones were poor. Hell, everybody was poor. They didn't have much land. Lots of 'em didn't have nothing. You kept 'em, and they worked for you. Almost every farm put up a colored family or old ones that didn't have no family, ones nobody couldn't help out. I kept many a one back in the thirties and forties, let 'em stay in the old houses. We even built one or two places for 'em, just little places, but they was dry and warm.

And they had their separate restaurants. In the store up here, he used to have a colored entrance. There were two sides to that place to eat or drink beer. One side had a sign on it said "Colored;" the other said "White." There was a little place cut out to hand things through between there.

In the movies – I saw an old movie poster just the other week. There was no date on there, but it was the "Treasure of the Sierra Madre" with Humphrey Bogart, and that was in the thirties I guess, late thirties or early forties, one. And that poster had on the bottom of it – I think it was the Shore Theater – it had a line said something like "nice balcony" or "clean balcony for the colored."

The old Indiantown Church was a pretty little church. It had a balcony they had made for slaves, but I never did

50

see no colored ones out there when we used to go there. Nobody sat in the balcony then. And just like the schools – the colored and the white didn't go to the same schools, not when I was going to school.

⅏

A fire in the house or the barn in the old days was a bad problem. It was gone. You'd just try and get out what stuff you could, set it in the yard somewhere, and you'd watch it burn. In town they had a two-wheel rig that you had to push and pump by hand. It had maybe fifty gallon of water. You'd get four or five head and push the thing to the fire and start pumping. You filled that thing up from a pitcher-head pump. You'd pump it in buckets and pour it in there. That was in town. If you lived in the country, you didn't have no chance.

When I lived in the old brick house there by Chicone, lightning struck the barn one time. We had a colored boy stayed with us, and he was out on the porch. He said, "Look there! The barn's on fire!" And sure enough she was. Seven mules and horses – I think it was one or two horses – and an old sow and a calf. We figured they got killed with the lightning. We stayed out there all night and watched so it don't catch none of the other buildings. When barns burnt in them days, it was mostly lightning.

■

The Land

"I can't pay taxes on what I got."

I carried this old man with me one day. I was thinking about buying a piece of land. I got a price, and I asked him what did he think about it. "Well," it was all he would say, "it ain't going nowhere."

❧

There was an old dirt road went down through the neck. They tell me that's the land where I was born. I come out when I was big enough to work – to hire out. I might of been six or seven. It used to be lovely in there.

I and my brother went back there with a Model T one time, and the road went all through that pine thicket – great big pines, and the mud up to your ass. Through them trees was the crookedest road I ever seen. You'd be in one of them trees in a heartbeat. You got down in them tracks with your wheels, and there weren't no way out, but we didn't get stuck. There was a old well in there, and we thought that's might be the place we were born.

❧

That old farm down there on the other side of where I was born and raised – a man from Virginia bought that for the trees. He cut the timber off it and said to my father, "I'll sell you both these farms for five thousand dollars."

My father said, "Lord no! I don't want it. I've already got more than enough as it is." Them farms would bring half a million dollars today.

❧

Back in the thirties this man had a farm up here – two hundred acres and a big house – and he had a mortgage on it for ten thousand dollars. He worried hisself to death that he'd lose it all for the taxes. He was worried to death. He sold it after a while for seventy-five thousand dollars, and then it sold later on for three hundred thousand. I don't know what it's worth today.

ะะ

That marsh I had – it was a sheriff's sale. That morning it was supposed to be sold at eleven o'clock. I hadn't thought much about it, but I said, "I've a great mind to ride down to the courthouse and see what goes."

The man put it up for sale, and somebody bid five hundred dollars. Then somebody went six, and somebody else went seven. I bid eight. It hang around and hang around, and in a few minutes he said, "Sold." Three hundred and forty-two acres.

I hunted that land in fall and winter and trapped it in spring for fifteen or twenty years, then I rented it out to a hunting club from Washington. I owned it for forty years, and somebody wanted to buy it. I said seventy-five thousand dollars, and that's what I got for it.

ะะ

Willie was born and raised back here, just the other side of Clyde's. He lived there for a long time. He offered that farm to me for five thousand dollars. Damn! You couldn't even make the taxes to pay for what I did have. Another place I was offered for seven thousand. Some boys just give two hundred thousand for it; yes sir, give two hundred thousand for it.

And up here where Perry lives, there's not much land to that, and it ain't worth nothing 'cause it's low and springy. You can get in the mire there anytime. I was driving a pump out here next to the ditch bank, and this man comes along.

He said, "Look, this place up here – we gotta do something with it." He said, "It's five thousand dollars against it is all."

I said, "Yeah, but I can't pay taxes on what I got, and I got to work day and night as it is."

There ain't a hundred acres in that whole thing, woods and all, and it's a hundred and seventy thousand if you want it now.

There's only one place I bought and sold again, and I give that away. It was a hundred and ten acres, and there was some old-growth pine on there, big old pines. I cut some, but there was one more big thicket back there. I give sixteen hundred for it.

I offered it to old man Ed Moore. I said, "You need a home, and I got more than I can do." I said, "I'll let you have that farm for eighteen hundred dollars."

He said, "Too much! I can't make enough to eat." But he'd put two horses to the wagon and drive clear down to town every day, and he'd set around there talking just as hard as he could talk, all day and all night till that store closed. I said, "Well, it's gonna be too much then. I ain't taking no less."

So I was out here cultivating along the road one day, and Kenny Hackett was hauling school children in his car. He owned two or three, and they were going to high school. He seen me out there and waited till I got to the end of the row. He said, "You got a place I can sell for you?"

I set there a minute or two. I said, "Yeah, you can sell that place over the road there."

He said, "What you want for it?"

I said, "Twenty-five hundred." I figured that would shut him up.

He said, "Well, that'll mean twenty-eight hundred."

I said, "I don't give a damn what you get."

I never thought no more about it till one day I come in, and Mary said, "Mr. Hackett said he sold the farm to a man from Chester. Said he'd come over here next week to straighten up for it." So he come down, and we straightened up for it.

Well, that man kept it for about six months and sold it to somebody from Philadelphia. And damn if he didn't sell it for thirty-seven hundred and fifty dollars. And it didn't stop there. That man got cancer and didn't live a year, and it went again. And I think Hackett was selling it every time and making two or three hundred every time he sold it.

જ

He paid a million dollars for that farm, and the land so poor it can't hatch a killdee egg.

જ

The land – the marsh and the woods – has been here for thousands and thousands of years, and I don't know why you have to do anything about it now. There's always some wise guy wants to change stuff around.

■

Farming

"Oh shit! It was awful times then."

I started farming with my father. He might of had thirty-five or forty acres. You could work that with horses and mules. Course we started early. It was some work to it. That's all there was to it, just work all the way around. You plant a piece in corn – I never thought I would get through with that. It was just something to do with that corn all the time. You would cultivate it till you couldn't see yourself in it, couldn't even see the mule, and the ears be hitting you in the face, and the blades cutting you. I've often wondered since why we didn't plant it closer, the way you do now, so all them weeds couldn't grow when it got high. You just done what everybody always done. We done what they call "other-rowed" it: You done every other row and come back and fill in three or four days later.

Before they got dry, you pulled the blades off. That was for feed. Blades was nice feed in that time. Then you cut the tops off and cut the stalk down. You had to cut that corn by hand, each stalk with a corn knife. There weren't no combines then, and you couldn't waste all the blades and the stalk. That was your feed for the winter.

You'd pile the stalks in piles and leave the ear on there. That ear wasn't ready yet, wasn't dry enough. It made better feed and was easier to cut when it was still green some. You'd shock the stalks up, and it would keep all winter. You just pulled it when you needed it, shuck the corn out, and haul it to the pound. It was something to do.

I'll never forget: I used to pick up the big ears and pile that to itself. Then I would go back and get the nubbins, them little, short corns, and pile that to theirselves. And you know: I done that when I first started on my own. A fellow said to me one day, "What you making two piles for? It's all eaten the same, ain't it?" Well, I stopped then, and I ain't done it again from that day to this day.

They had it all mapped out so you had plenty of work. There weren't no chance to work half a day and get some whiskey and get drunk. You didn't have time for that.

It really tickled me though: When you planted corn then, you planted four or five grains in a hill. Then you'd go back and pull out two or three – go all over that field bending down, pull out two or three, and leave two grains there. Price of seed today, can you see pulling up half what you plant? I told 'em it was something wrong with that to start with.

They told me, "Oh, you just don't want to do no work nohow." That's what they told me.

I used to hate that job, I really hated that. That's one job I hated. It was enough to make a preacher cuss. I said, "That's something wrong with this. I don't know what it is, but it's something wrong. Ain't supposed to do like that."

After that they got a sleigh. That's when the advances come out. You hooked a mule to the sleigh and drive along and thinned out the corn like that. You wouldn't have to bend your back so much. It was fancy stuff in that time. It was a sleigh with a top. You hooked a mule to it, and he'd pull it.

The scent of pulling them stalks made me sick to my stomach. I'd get to vomit. The scent of that corn give me a sick headache and a sick stomach, just sick as a dog, but I'd keep on. The old mule just creeping along, and you setting on this sleigh. Every time you get to a hill, you're right to another one. It was supposed to be four foot apart, but it looked like one was on top of the next.

They planted in hills, four or five seed to a hill, and it was supposed to be four feet from one hill to the next. It was later on that people started planting corn one grain to each spot, close together. Oh shit! It was awful times then.

ॐ

The way you hook a mule to a plow: First you get that bridle on him so you can handle him a little bit. Bring him out and put the collar on him; fasten that and get your harness hanging up there. Most of 'em had chain traces to pull by, but I got one set down to the barn that's leather. They're hooked on the hames, and you put the hames on his collar. There's a ridge around the collar, and the chain hooks on the side. Then you got a cloth band about as wide as your hand, and that goes over his back, right back of his shoulders, to hold those traces up. That holds 'em up so he ain't stepping out of 'em when you're turning. You got a hook on the end that hooks into the singletree. Then, when you got him hooked up, you get your reigns on him. The hook on the back of the singletree hooks into the plow. If you got three mules, then it's called a tripletree – three teams side by side. Most of the time you got leather reins, but you can use ropes. Then he's ready to go.

ॐ

When I was six, my father put me in the field to the cultivator. We had what you called "Fluke Hair." It was V shaped and had three flukes on there, one up front, one in the middle, and one on the back. You'd cultivate half the row at a time, and we always cultivated right-handed, had the teeth set for the right side of the row. You'd go down the right side and come back that same row, but you're cultivating the right row each way. You used one mule or one horse to it.

My father said, "Get out there and cultivate." I was a little fellow, and I had to reach way up there to get that handle. Pretty soon I turned around and was cultivating the left side where there wasn't the right teeth. My father said,

"I want you to cultivate like I told you. I don't want to tell you again." I done it right after that.

After a while they got to make ones with five teeth, and then they made ones you could ride. I used a pair of mules then, and it straddled the row. It had things you could put your feet on to steer it with.

ʃæ

We used to plant corn with the dogwood storms, with all them storms you have in April. You see a dogwood blossom then, "Man, it's time to plant corn."

We would check plant: plant it like a checkerboard so you could cultivate either way. It got more room to grow, and you could cultivate it easier. We planted Lancaster corn; they called it flint corn. It had some colors in it like Indian corn, but it wasn't Indian corn. It didn't yield much like today. Maybe you'd get thirty or thirty-five bushels to the acre. I don't guess nobody plants that no more.

You plowed whenever you could from March on, whenever it was dry enough to get on the land. We started with a single, fourteen-inch plow, and we hooked up anywhere from two to three mules depending on how hard the ground was. You walked behind the plow and held on to the handles. Later on we had a double plow. You rode on that one – four mules hooked to the double.

We had all kinds of drags with spikes out of 'em. They'd scratch the ground up after you plowed. After we got tractors, we had an old iron drag to break up the clots. If it was real clotty – if you plowed when it was a little wet – well, then you might run a roller over it. Nora used to drive her father's ox with a roller.

At first you had to plant with a hoe – most did that. You'd dig a little hole and throw the seed in there. The women used to help us with that. You marked off your rows across the field with a stick marker. You used a eight-foot plank with shoes on it: a piece of two-by-four

59

bolted down there every four feet. It marked off three rows at a time. You hooked a horse to that and dragged it across the field after the ground was worked. Then you would walk along that row and chop out a hill with your hoe every four feet and plant the seed.

Next we had a planter that ran on a wire. It was like a telephone wire, and it had a knot out there every four feet to trip the planter. It was just as long as the field. It was cut and tied together – that's the way it looked like it was done. The farmer didn't do that; they did it where you bought it at. You'd stretch that wire all the way across a forty-acre field and drive in a stob at each end to hold it. The planter ran over the wire, and the wire tripped the planter to drop seed every four foot. It would drop four or five seed at a time. Sometimes that old wire would break, and then you'd have to walk clean back to the end, pull the stob up, and fix your wire. Then you went back and hammered the stob back in. You better stick it back in the same hole or your rows wouldn't be even. After you finish one row, then you move the stobs over four feet and start another row. It was work to get it straight across that forty acres, and you wanted the rows even both ways so you could cultivate in either direction. You rolled the wire up on a reel after you got done planting and put it away. The old wire would get rotten after you had it several years and would break a lot.

Pop used to have me put out chicken manure by each hill, scoop a little out there by each hill. After it started to grow, it got them suckers. I had to cut 'em off, hoe 'em off or chop 'em. All that green corn juice – it sure did smell.

I found a box of old husking pegs down to the barn not long ago. Now that was a job I don't miss neither. You needed that peg to get into the cap on the corn when it was dried. That cap was growed around there pretty tight sometimes. That peg cut into the cap and gets it started for you to pull her back. "The Boss" was the best peg we ever had, with that offset hook, but there was all kinds. Lots made their own. You could carve a point on some little stick and put a leather tab or a cord on there. That would go around your fingers to hold her on there. They had some pretty fancy patents, but "The Boss" was the best one I ever had.

We used to do ten barrels a day – one person – and it's ten bushels to a barrel. But we didn't use no barrel; that's just what they used to call it. Now it's all by the bushel or by weight, and nobody leaves the cob on no more. You just go out there with the combine and shell it while you cut it. But back then you cut it and shocked it up, and then you went back to that shock to husk it.

When the corn got ripe enough, and you think it'll keep, you go out there with the corn knife and chop it down. I would sweat blood then. I'd cut a while and shock a while. Many years I cut forty acres with just a corn knife.

Then, later on, I got a one-row cutter. It had a little body on there. It wasn't over four feet long and three feet high, and maybe four feet wide. It was open. It had a blade down there and one wheel to the front. That wheel let the old mule turn at the row end and come back in another row. It had bigger wheels for the back where the body and the corn was. You drive along, and this blade cuts that stalk off, and you throw it back in the body. There was a cutter blade bolted on a piece of wood. It was kind of cattybiasoned. God, if that weren't something: you a-sweating, and the corn slapping you side of the head. And if that corn got real dry, that blade would pull it up instead of cutting it. It was a right smart patent. You were setting on there, and it had the body right behind. It weren't right back of you but a little past, and you'd knock the corn stalks back in there. The ears and stalks was way to the back part and made it heavy. It had a little trip you put your foot on when you got ready to dump the body. You get off against the pile where you want to drop it, and you just trip that thing, and the stalks would come off.

You piled up a place on the ground, and after you got your pile so you thought it was right, you set it up. Then you tied a string around it, and you had your shock.

Then you get your wheat planted or whatever you needed to do, and then you went back and start husking. You go out there to the shock and husk it right there in the field. You untie your string – it was a piece of old binding twine – and you lay it out there somewheres where you can find it, 'cause you wanted to tie that shock up again after you get the corn out. You pull one stalk out at a time and husk her; make a pile right there on the ground; throw them cobs right out there.

You come for it later with a wagon. You had a shoveling board you put on the tailboard of the wagon, and that gives you a place to start with the shovel, to shovel it right down that board into the wagon. Then you haul it up and throw it in the cornhouse, pile it way over your head.

We had forty acres we had to do that way. After you husk all that corn out, you would shock the fodder back up, right there in the field, and from then on you'd just go back out there when you wanted to feed it. We finally wound up with a little cart, a two-wheeled cart. You'd put two horses to it and back it right up against that shock. That cart would break out at the tongue; the tongue of it tilted. You back them horses right up against that shock and put a rope around it. You had a piece of pipe mounted on the wagon, and you put the rope around that and crank the shock right on the cart. Then you carry the whole thing to the pound. All you had to do was loosen that rope up and it's fall right off. You scatter that fodder around a little after you dumped it off in the pound, and the stock would eat that.

Some had a little sled to haul fodder out of the field. I used that once when I started. You used to pull the sled behind you. It didn't have no wheel, but it was like the first kind of wheelbarrow. Later on they put a wheel on it, and then you pushed it ahead of you.

We had a corn crusher for the cows. I run that with the tractor and crushed the corn up, cob and everything. You had a box in every stable, and you pour a quart or so in when you milk. You use them little short ears in there – they called 'em nubbins – and damaged corn. But most of it you feed right on the cob.

In the spring you'd sell your extra corn. Mace had a sheller what run on a tractor. You shovel it right into her, and she'd shell it. He done most of the shelling around here. It had wheels on it, something like a wheat thrasher, and you pull it from one farm to the others.

Course everybody had a little sheller. Some of 'em used to be double: put an ear of corn in two holes instead of one. All farmers or those who lived in the country some-wheres had a sheller for the chickens and ducks. They're nice to hull walnuts with too.

We didn't plant much soybean. They planted it for feed then, cut it when it was green and let it cure. They called it soybean hay.

We planted lots of wheat and some barley and rye too. I've thrashed wheat till I seen stars. Some, if they had just a little patch, would use an old flail. It was two sticks with some leather strap or rope to hold 'em together, so one could swing on the other. You hold onto one stick, the long one, and you swing the short one around and beat them stalks. After you beat all that kernels out, then you throw it up in the wind. The wind blows off the chaff, and the kernel fall back down so you can shovel it in a bag. That was some work to it.

I had a machine. I thrashed all the wheat around here one time, anybody had a little patch. I pulled it with the old Farmall tractor. It had a great, long belt you run be-tween the tractor and that old rig. I sold it after everybody got a combine.

Some of 'em would take and ride horses. They'd get

them big-footed Perchins with them great big feet and ride 'em up and down over that stalks of wheat, and that would shell it out.

We started to cut wheat with a scythe, and it had a cradle on there to catch it. Then you tie up a bundle with some wheat straw and shock them bundles up till you thresh it out. But when the binder come out, we bought a brand new one. That thing was hard to pull though; had to use three mules to it. We didn't have no tractor then, just seven horses and mules that time. It had a sickle blade that would cut the wheat, and when it got so much in there, it tied it in a bunch. After you got five bunches, it had a trip would dump 'em. It was six, seven foot maybe. Then you had somebody come along and pick up them bunches and shock it. There'd be ten or fifteen bunches in one shock. When the shock was done, you took two bunches and spraddled it all out from where the string was around the middle, spraddle it, and make a cap to keep the rain off.

After it set there and dried – course it got wet and dried half a dozen times – the wheat thrasher come in. All the neighbors would help one another and haul them bundles to the thrasher. After it beat the kernels out and throwed the straw up in a pile, then you hauled it and put it in the barn, or sometimes you'd haul it to the station and put it in a rail car.

Clay Webb bought wheat for some mill over in Berlin. There was no way to test it for moisture and all that then. He'd bite it and see how the kernel was. If it was right, he'd give you so much and load it on the train. They had a siding there, and they'd put a car on it for him.

The thrashers started out with steam, but it went to gas about '32. You used to have to cut wood for the steam engine at first. You had this steam engine: it was all in one machine like a tractor, but it went mighty slow. It was twice, three times as big as a tractor, and it had a great, long belt. You'd set your thrashing machine off there, and then you'd come out here to the end of that belt with the engine. It was a long ways from the steam engine to the thrasher, and you'd run the thrashing machine with that long belt. You couldn't get too close with the engine 'cause it was fired with wood. It had a screen to go over the stack, but shit, the sparks would come out of there. When it was just about dark and you run that thing, man, you talk about fire coming out. They burned up a lot of straw ricks. They tried to set that engine so it would be side to the wind and wouldn't blow the sparks back on the rick. You had to figure out something or you'd burn 'em up every time. You had to haul water to that thing with a fifty gallon barrel. You had to pump it by hand, and just an old mule with a sled to pull it out to the steam engine. You had another barrel out there, and you just bucket it from one over to the other and go back and fill 'er up again.

You took your mule and wagon and went around and helped all the neighbors. Damn! I loaded – I think it was seven wagons one morning. Wasn't a damn soul that time but me would help this man. I think it was seven wagons, and not a soul to throw up wheat but me. I throwed up every binder from the shocks to fill them seven wagons. My brother had an old Model T truck and was hauling wheat, and he stopped by. Boy, it was hot that morning. I was right on the edge of the road when he come along. He said, "Why don't you slack up?"

I said, "Damn, there ain't neither another soul out here to help." I said, "I gotta do something." So I finished loading that wagon.

He said, "I'll bring you a Coca Cola when I come back from town."

I remember when I lived down below Mardela on a farm – I was just a kid. The wheat thrasher that come there didn't have no blower on it. It just thrashed out the wheat, and the straw fell right down behind the machine. I seen Pop and different ones take an old mule and hook it to a rail, same like you had for a fence, and tie a rope or chain to each end of it so you could pull it. He'd drive that old mule up on the straw, lay that rail behind it, and pull it out. Sometimes they'd tack a board on the rail to give you a chance to stand on there and hold it down. But after they got that blower, it would blow the straw right straight out there or anywhere you wanted it.

I got my first tractor when I was in the cordwood business. It didn't have no rubber tires on it; it had them old spiked wheels.

But the first thing I had was a Sears Roebuck rig. I went out to Corkran's one day to look at theirs, and it was doing a good job. I said, "I've a great mind to order one." Up till then it was horses or mules. The old horse I had at that time wasn't worth five cents. He wouldn't pull the hat off your head, so I got one.

I bought an old used Model A roadster, and I sent off to Sears Roebuck and got that stuff. A hundred and some dollars, a hundred and fifteen I think. You take the body off this car and use that frame, and you bolt on that rig. It was a axle and spiked wheels and some cogs and other stuff. It was all out in the open; I mean it wasn't closed in like tractors now are. They had this great big cog fastened to that wheel and a little cog fastened to your axle on the Model A, and that's what drove the thing. Everything was iron on the back, and I used that for years.

I got the ground in down the road with that rig. That whole field was growed up. There was pines in there big enough for the mill and plenty bushes. I pulled and pulled 'em, but every once in a while she'd wring the axle off that little cog. She had a lot of power, and that Model A axle wasn't strong enough to drive all that stuff. I broke seven or eight axles. I'd have to look up an old one and stick it in there.

Later on I'd go back in the swamp and haul wood all winter. It got so bad in there, I made a great, wooden sled with runners on it for the snow and mud. I could haul half a cord with it. I cut a hundred or so cord every winter and sold it for seventy-five cents or a dollar a cord. You cut it with a ax, and then I cut it with a saw in stove length.

I remember an old tractor that Pop had. I got stuck with that thing every time I went out there. Pop told me: "I'd rather have a pair of Perchin horses than that thing." He got her sunk one time on the back place. That old land – you'd go right along just as nice as anything, and all at once you'd fall through. He come to shoveling it out, and I went back there to see what he was doing. He got so mad trying to shovel her out; he took that shovel and started piling dirt right on top of that hood. He buried her.

Before you had all them rigs and tractors, you just grubbed out the roots with mules or horses, or you hired a bunch, and they'd dig with grubbing hoes, just dig up the whole thing. The horses and the mules didn't like that job much. Them old horses Pop had would bite you if you didn't watch 'em, and the old mule would bite you too, but mostly he'd try to kick the shit out of you. Old Jim was working up here and got a pair of mules in the mire. He went around to their head, and one bit him. They had to take his leg off. Them old mules can be bad. They're down there clean to their bellies, and they want to get out. If they can't get up, they'll grab any straw they see.

I had all this grubbed up around here. Had one fella come out – he'd come up here and get his 'baccer and go out there with his grubbing hoe. I give him so much to grub up a certain place. He'd dig all around them big old stumps and dig them roots out. He'd be two or three days getting one stump out, but he'd finally get 'er. He'd take the old horses and haul it around in a pile. Then he'd dig all the dirt out of the stumps. Man, it was a job. It was that.

I hear some places they would use them old stumps for a fence, drag 'em in a row for a fence. Could-a-done, but we never done that here. All we ever had was rail fences in them days. When we moved up to that old farm in Indian-town in 1920, that had a rail fence all the way around, and they partitioned off in the middle with a rail fence. That's what we had around all the farms in the early days. It was made crossed up, one rail on the other, and zigzagged. They had a post there in the middle where the rails crossed. The post set between the rails on the outside. That locks 'em, and that post stops the cows and horses from pushing off the rails. Them rails were twelve, fifteen foot, all split and real light – walnut and cypress. I guess that fence be worth a million dollars today with the price of walnut, and there ain't no more cypress. We burned 'em in the stove when we took 'em down. I'll tell you – you talk about a hot fire. My God! The whole thing was, though, you had to keep toting in wood just as fast as you could. We had rails piled up everywhere in that yard. I guess we took a whole year getting that fence down. I mean it weren't all year, just in the wintertime and what time we weren't doing other chores.

Them were some days. You tell the kids about it, and they don't believe you. So a man could plant thirty, forty acres with some help. We had the horses and the mules. There was Pop and my brother and myself, three of us, and sometimes we'd hire somebody, one, or maybe two for a while. And now one farmer plants three thousand, four thousand acres with some help, and he ain't no better off than we were, just owes more money.

ε

The way I would make a corn shock: I would start at one corner of the field and walk down four rows or hills. You could go more or less; depends how big you want your shock. I would walk over four rows and start in the field. I'd walk in there four rows and take and bend four hills together and tie 'em up. You make like a tent from the four hills. Now you keep on down that row, and you cross over

68

and tie up the hills every eight hills. This will be your shocks; this is what you pile the stalks against to make your shock.

Now you take your corn knife and start back down that row. You cut the stalks and pile 'em up in your arm till you get to the place where your shock is. You pile up what you cut against one side. You go on and cut four rows in each direction from there and pile it against the shock. It's a square of eight hills by eight hills with the shock in the middle. You cut and pile it against there, a little on each side to keep it balanced, to keep it from pushing over. When you have the shock finished, you take a stalk and twist it around near the top of the shock. You can bend it at the sections and stick them under, like tie it together. If it's still green enough, it will twist around and hold it. If you can't make that hold, you can tie it with baling twine. You do that all the way across the field. Then you start with another row till you cut the whole field. Eight hills by eight hills makes one shock. It's some work to it, and that's just the start. You got to come back later and husk the ears and tote 'em in. And you tote the fodder in when you need it for feed or to put in the barn.

a.

It was a big business years ago to cut sawgrass off the marsh. They would cut it with a scythe, just like you cut wheat or hay, and they would load it on scows and send it to Baltimore. They packed bananas or produce or something in it. You could use it for hay too, but it weren't too sporty for feed.

You could drive out across the hard parts of the marsh then, but it's too wet now. Captain George Richardson said he drove a Model T right across Savanna Lake in 1903 or 1904, somewhere about there. He said it was a dry year, and the ground was dry and cracked open. The tide rises and falls in there now, but there weren't no inlet then.

I put out a couple row of 'taters this week, something for the bugs. When I was plowing out there, it turned up some old, hard-shelled 'tater bugs, turned 'em right out of the ground. He just spent the whole winter in there, the whole bug. Now I had a time about that.

The only way I found to be sure you kill him is to get a brickbat and lay it on the ground. Then you get the bug and you lay him down on that brickbat. Then you take another brickbat and "clap!" He's gone then.

Somebody paid five dollars for that, sent away and got it. The ad said, "Guaranteed to kill potato bugs." Said to send five dollars for a sure kill. They didn't even send him the brickbats; they just sent him what to do. That's the truth. It was in a magazine.

&

This stuff they do now in the canning houses: it's a wonder it don't kill everybody. They start with the tomato plant. It's been sprayed for this, that, and the other before it ever comes to you to put in the field. Then they spray the ground, and they spray the plants again for this, that, and everything else. Then they turn around and kill the vines with another spray. They pick 'em and carry 'em to the canning house and put 'em through lye. Some places they turn gas on 'em. I seen this man putting lye in them tomatoes, and he says it eats the soles right off his shoes, eats the soles right off! And finally they puts the tomato in a can, and they tell you that none of that gets in there. It goes through half a dozen or ten things what got skulls and crossbones on the side of the box, right on there! And they put them tomatoes on these pizzas. Everybody likes 'em, I guess so, but not me. I'll never get used to that, not after it goes through all that stuff.

&

I thought about old man Moore the other day. He'd rent every place there was to plant and wouldn't raise nothing. He rented a place one year and planted seven bushels of wheat. When it come on ripe, he cut it and shocked it, and the wheat thrasher come in to thrash. He got exactly seven bushels, just what he planted.

But I can't say nothing about him this year; I was worse than that. I paid two hundred and ninety-one dollars for corn seed, and I got two hundred and twenty-one out of it. And that don't count the fertilizer and spray and all that. I done better with horses, and I didn't want to plant no corn nohow.

&

People don't plant much by the signs no more. I got a book that's pretty good, and I plant a lot by that. It don't stand on the moon too much, but it gives you all the signs. Now the breast sign is one of the best for planting. Then there's some will plant by the tide, with the tide coming in. Well, that comes in and out two times every day, but you want to start with it coming in. Some say that's just superstition, but the old ones knew better.

&

Talk about superstitions, good Lord help my soul. My father had a certain day to do everything, and he wouldn't do nothing on a Friday. He had a certain day to plant corn, a certain day to plant potatoes. It used to make me so mad: I was almost growed and want to go somewhere fourth of July in the afternoon, and he'd have to plant late potatoes. No other day in the world you could plant 'em.

&

Old man Hughes lived down to Hurleys Neck. He had to plant his potatoes on St. Patrick's Day. Said if you didn't plant 'em on St. Patrick's Day, you wouldn't grow none. He lived down in that low land and never growed as many as he planted, but he planted 'em every year on St. Patrick's Day. He never gave up on it.

҈

My pop wouldn't work a team on a Friday. You could do something else – ride 'em around if you want – but he never would work 'em as a team. That was bad luck.

The old fella lost all his money one time. He was plowing on a Friday. His wallet worked out of his coveralls, and he plowed it under. But he got it back. When he plowed the next year, he found it. Course it was all rotted and everything in there. Some lawyer sent it off to Washington and got his money back, but he never did no more plowing on a Friday.

҈

Gosh sake, all the old people had bean day. They'd look at the almanac – twin day was the best. They always planted 'em that day, pole beans especially.

I missed bean day this year, but you know what you can do: If you can't plant 'em when the moon is right, you just put 'em in a jar that day and bury the jar. Then you can dig it up anytime you want, and they'll be O.K. You can plant 'em anytime then. You gotta have the right moon or you got nothing.

҈

I had watermelons one year, and it come up a real dry spell. Something kept eating 'em up, and Pop said it was rabbits. I said, "Aw, it can't be."

"Yeah, that's what it is," he says.

So I went down one night, and they was all over out there, little old things, big ones, and everything else. I said, "Well!"

Pop says, "If you kill one and pull him apart, and if

you strew him all up and down beside the woods where they come out at, that blood and stuff will keep him away."

That night I went out there and shot one, 'bout two-thirds growed. I put my foot on him and pull him apart. I go up a little farther and pull some more of him off and drag him up and down there. They never come out no more after that. I don't know if that kept 'em away or if they were just tired of coming out there.

■

Domestic Animals

"The preacher would bless them dogs
every Sunday."

The ox, now given his mind, could be just as stubborn as the old mule. Whenever he got hot and caught sight of some branch or ditch with water into it, well now, you get ready to get your feet wet. He was in there.

Sometimes, if he got tired and you let up on the whip, he'd lay right down there, and it was one time to get him up again. There was an old fellow said he knew just what to do: "You just look around and find yourself a big old bullfrog. You prys that ox's mouth open and throws in that old bullfrog. He's up then." He told more, but I can't remember the rest. He told a lot of stuff, that old man done.

Sometimes they would build a fire under him, right there against his hide. You heard that old saying: "build a fire under him." Well, that's just what they done.

Mr. Handley died not long ago. He still used oxen. He was the last one around here. He belonged in another time.

૨૦

A lot of people used steers instead of oxen in the old days. Them oxen are just so slow, but they can get around in the woods and the marsh. They got feet just like a duck; it spreads out. A mule now, he'll fall right through.

૨૦

When I lived over the way there, a fellow used to come by on a Sunday morning with a steer hooked up to his carriage, and him sitting back there just trotting along. He had a harness on him just the same you would have on a horse. Now that was a strange sight.

≈

Wilbur had a old sawmill back here one time, and it come winter, and he couldn't work back there. He had this yoke of steers, and he asked Pop if he could keep the steers with our cows. He told Pop he'd pay him, and Pop said to turn 'em out in the pound.

Well, I was hauling manure one day, and I decided to hook up them steers to the wagon. I thought I was big then; I was seventeen, maybe eighteen. You spread the manure out of the wagon then with a fork instead of a manure spreader. So I loaded her up and got on top of that wagon, and I was talking to them steers. We get out there in the middle of the pasture field, and we're going along just nice, and all of a sudden this one steer falls right out. I said, "My gosh! Damn! I done killed the man's steer." I got off and looked at him, and his eyes were rolled right up there. I touched him with the whip, and he started to getting up, and I seen the chain was choking him. I didn't have no weight on the tongue, and that's what he pulled by. I knowed what to do then. I didn't let nobody know about it though. I just put them steers back in the pound and got the mules. It scared me.

≈

There was an old man over here one time had a steer and wanted to break it. Trouble was: he didn't have but one steer, and he had a double yoke. So he told his wife, "I'm going to yoke myself beside this steer, and you take the straps." And he done it. They said it like to kill that old man.

≈

If you want to work a steer now, you got to trim him, or else he sees a cow and takes right off. You have to cut him. My uncle used to do that for farmers all around here. He was a good veterinarian in his day, and I used to help him. I was his helper from the time I was twelve years old. If anything had to be done, like a bull, I had to hold him while he take his nuts out. I've done it hundreds of times.

We had a man lived down here, and he had a bull. He wanted him castrated. We went over there and tied him up and cut his nuts out. Just about the time we got done cutting, the whistle blew down to the steam mill: twelve o'clock.

The old man said, "Oh my God! He'll die a-for sundown." He said, "The moon's due south at twelve o'clock. He'll die a-for sundown sure."

My uncle up and left. He thought that was funny.

But the old man told him the next day, "He died just about five o'clock yesterday afternoon."

That was a big, strong bull, and he died before sundown. The old man didn't miss it. We used to have some awful times about that.

&

We went down to Hurleys Neck one time. They had a bull in this pound, and there was a big, pine-slab fence went all the way around her. Old Mr. Crockett come to watch. He had a great old coat on and was walking with his cane. He could just about get around with that cane.

I tied that bull up, all four legs to a post. When we was done castrating, I took the lines off him, and he just laid there. He was mad. We all got outside the fence, but Mr. Crockett stayed in there with that bull. After a spell he took his cane and spiked that bull in the ribs. That bull jumped right up and made for the old man. Well now, Mr. Crockett throwed away his cane and flew; run right up to that fence and jumped right over the top of it. He got the cure quick.

&

The thing I didn't like the most was sawing the horns off a bull or a cow. You used to take a hand saw and saw 'em right off. I want to tell you: that was barbarous. My lord, you take a bull, and he'd have a fit. I don't care how big and wild he was; when you take him down and start sawing his horns off, he has a fit. You better have him tied good. You got to have him tied all four feet to a gate post or something.

&

If a cow be in labor a day or two and couldn't have her calf – its head back and its feet in the wrong place – my uncle would say, "I can fix that." He'd roll up his sleeves and go right into that cow. He'd take the calf and push him back, straighten his feet out, and he'd get him starting out of there. I've seen him do it over and over again.

&

You take a female hog now, when she'd get into heat and run around the bushes and rip everything up, well, they'd call my uncle.

Nelson would say, "I'll fix her. Take her over and let me get to her." He'd have to take her ovaries out. We called them pig bags. I'd get her back legs pried open. I'd hold onto her, and he'd open her up. He'd take his little knife and trim them huckleberries right off, cut every one of 'em right off.

You see, she'd got little bags in there where the little pigs form in every one that's ripe at that time. She may have four; she may have six; she may have eight. You could tell how many pigs she was going to have by counting those with the black knots on 'em. That's what he called huckleberries. You cut them huckleberries off, and she wouldn't go into heat anymore.

After he'd take his knife and slice 'em off, he'd sew her back up. He always had a crooked needle with thread into it, and he'd sew her up with that. He'd put a little pine tar on her and let her go. That wound it up. "She's all right now," he'd say. He done that all over the place. Anybody had that kind of trouble, they called him.

☙

This man had a sheep one time that had some lambs. One of the lambs had a brown spot back there, but there wasn't any hole under the tail, and he kept drinking milk. He swelled up and swelled up and swelled up some more. The man called up Nelson, and he said, "What are we gonna do?"

Nelson said, "I'll fix him up." He took his knife and just cut a swipe across there. Man, the stuff flew out of that lamb.

Four or five days later, Nelson asked the man how was the lamb.

Man said, "He died."

Nelson said, "Oh my Lord, I forgot to put a drawing string into it."

☙

A fellow lived down to the woods one time, and he went and got a horse, bought it from down below town. He got that horse home, and it weren't feeling right, so he gets this old man to come and take a look. He was supposed to be a veterinarian. He come down and taps a whole lot of blood out. He was drawing blood right out.

This fella says, "Look here now; stop that! I don't want it to die." He seen all that blood out there. So the old man stopped it.

Two, three days later I seen him. I said, "How is your horse doing?"

He said, "All right."

I said, "He done got all right did he?"

"Yes sir," he says, "and I got a pretty little colt there

to the barn too."

⁊ₐ

If a mule or a hoss balked, you used a twitch on 'em. You put that on an old mule's nose and tighten it up – I'll tell you one thing: he'd shape up then. I've seen 'em twist his ear up with one too. For bulls you had a bull cinch. It's a ring on a shaft. You put the ring in his nose, and you hold him off with the shaft. You could stick a ring in his nose and snap a rope into it, and you could lead him with that, but with just the ring he could run around you and anyway at all.

We had a wheat thrashing over to the brick-house farm one time. Old John had a pair of horses there, and you couldn't get 'em up to that thrasher – the belt and all that machinery running, you know. The old horses just balked. John tied a string around their ears and twitched it up there tight. Them horses went right up there then.

I got a twitch down to the barn. It's a shovel handle so there's something to put your hand in, and the other end has a rope through a hole. If he wouldn't go somewhere or do something, you get hold of that old mule and put that rope around his upper lip and twist it. It would make him say his prayers.

⁊ₐ

One of the greatest jobs was castrating a tomcat. Now he'd get you. What you had to do was take a boot, put him down in that boot, and then put his back legs through them loops where you pull your boots on. Then you castrate him.

People used to bring cats for Pop to castrate, and I used to hold 'em. He was quick. He'd cut them nuts right out of there, throw some ashes on it, and let him go. Moon had to be right though. I don't remember just how that was, where the moon had to be, but I know he wanted the moon in a certain place.

But old Saul said he didn't do that. He said, "What I do is to take a pair of scissors, hold him up by the nuts, clip 'em off, and let him fall." That boy could tell some awful tales.

≈

When you raised chickens in the old days, you had a lot of trouble with hen hawks, and the fox would get his share. But the old weasel was the worst. When the weasel came, he killed every one of 'em. He wouldn't eat 'em, just kill 'em and suck the blood all out of 'em.

≈

The foxes used to get Mom's chickens. There was a den out there in a thicket behind the house. We dug it up two or three times, but they'd just go back and make another one. Then, when they raised up their young ones, they'd come for the chickens.

I had to get up early to milk, and one morning I seen the old fox come trotting around the pasture. I took my gun and went out there. It was a long shot for the shotgun, but he tumbled right over. Pop sure hated that. He liked to run them old foxes with his dogs; Paul too. They had fifteen or eighteen dogs there one time, and the preacher would bless them dogs every Sunday.

≈

Mom used to raise up a few chickens when we lived over to the other farm. She had a little coop there, and the old hen hawk was getting her chickens like everything.

Now we didn't have time to set there all day and wait for this chicken hawk, but at dinner time we'd get our shotguns. One would set for a while and then the other for the dinner hour, but we never could get a shot. It didn't come.

Then one day – it was about eleven-thirty, and we hadn't come in from the fields yet – Mom said she heard something hit the side of the house. This hawk come after a chicken there in the yard, and he dived for it and struck the house. Mom got to the door, and it was turning 'round and 'round there by the stoop. She didn't have a thing to hit it with, so she pulled off her slipper and hit him over the head and killed him. There we was, setting out there all them days with a shotgun, and she kills him with a slipper. Damn if that didn't beat all I ever heard.

I'm lost since my pony died. Gosh sakes, I ain't got nothing to feed the scraps to. Every time she seen me she'd wicker; she'd think I had something for her. She'd eat all the stuff we had. I think it was asparagus and string beans she didn't like. Everything else she would eat. But I'm glad she went this way. She never made a squall. She never moved a foot when she fell. Her feet were just there. It didn't look like she ever made one kick. I hope I die that easy. I guess I'll have to get a goat or something.

■

81

Butchering Hogs

"You got to keep him chewing."

Used to be everybody had a hog. We used to butcher some big hogs. In them days everybody's neighbor would try to beat the other one, try to have the biggest hog and get all that lard and stuff out of it. But you didn't want to kill a hog while she was in heat; the meat wasn't too good then. And you didn't want to kill no boar hog nohow, lest not until he was castrated. Damn! You couldn't even stay in the house with it if you cooked that.

My father used to be great about butchering, and all the neighbors would come and help you, and you'd go and help them. Used to see hogs hanging all over. You don't see it nowadays.

It was some work into it. First you had to scald him. You set a barrel in the ground, say against a pound fence or something. You dig a slanting hole to put the barrel in and put some pine shats or straw out in front to pull him on. They had a pot out there, and they boiled water in it and poured it in this barrel. You got to get the water just right. You get it too hot and set that hair, man, you got a real job. The old folks would take a corn cob and stick it in there and read it: "Just about right." Then you put him in, one end or the other. You couldn't get the whole hog in. You don't keep him in too long. You pull him out after a little and let him get some air, and you pull on the hair to see if it come out good. You had to put a little more hot water in now and then when it would cool. You could pull a lot of hair by your hand. Then you take this scraper and scrape it back and forth to get the rest. People went around later on and killed 'em for other people, and they had a scalder, a great, long tub. They could lay the whole hog right in there.

Then you'd have hog hooks. I still got a few out to the barn. When you went to put him in that barrel, you'd put the hooks into the strings in his legs, or you'd put one of 'em in his mouth – snatch her right in there – so you have something to hold onto. You couldn't pull him by an old, slippery leg. It's just the same like a hay hook; you could use 'em for one thing or the other. I got one in my boat now. I got it tied to the front seat by a string. When I go perching, all I do is put the hook in the edge of some grass – the string's about three feet – and it'll hold you right there to the bank.

After you got him all scraped, then you hang him on the shear poles. That's what they call 'em; I don't know where they got that name from. You just line up three poles and bore a hole through the tops, and you put all three on this bolt. You lay them poles down side by side and put a bolt through them holes, kind of loose so you can spread 'em apart a little. You had some kind of peg drove in there on the two side poles, down below the bolt, for to hang the hog on. You swing the middle pole around so it sticks in the other direction, and you prys the two end ones apart so you can get the hog in there between 'em. You cut his heel strings open and stick 'em on them pegs. Then you take this pole you laid out in front, and you start to pick him up and pick him on up. One would get on each pole and push him up a little at a time. You'd pick the whole mess up, walk it right up. God sakes! You take a four or five hundred pound hog, you need something to get him up there. After you got him up there, then you prys the poles open so you can get in there and gut him. You gut him good and prop him open. What you do is to shave off a sassprus branch and stick it in there; let him cool out. If you'd skin all the bark off them poles and put 'em away in the barn or someplace, they'd last for years and years.

Anyway, after he's all cool, you cut him up, make all that lard and scrapple and everything. It was some work into it.

৯

Charlie was up there helping Pop kill hogs one time. They raised anywhere up to four, five, six hogs to killing time. They cut a couple of posts – I say posts – with a fork into 'em, and they cut another long post and lay it in them forks. Then they hang the hogs up on that, all in a row. Everybody had gone to eat dinner, and one of them hogs fell down. That hog would weigh five hundred pounds, and it fell down. Charlie – he was a big man anyway – he said, "Look, I'll hold him up there, and you hook his heel strings." He took that hog laying on the ground and lifted him right up there.

৯

We used to help the Frases kill hogs. We lived right beside of 'em. And Miss Frase – when you go to shoot a hog and go to cut his throat – she'd run out there with a bowl to catch all that blood. She'd make blood pudding with it. God! I couldn't stand that.

৯

My pop used to kill a mess of hogs and sugar cure it, you know, mix sugar and salt and rub it in there good. Some would smoke it. The Krafts – they were Germans – they used to smoke theirs. I had a book on sugar curing meat, a whole book on it. I used to slice the ham and cure it about a week. Pop used to use three cups of salt to a cup of brown sugar and a good pinch of black pepper, but what I did with mine was to mix two cups of dark brown sugar, one cup of salt – maybe a couple of teaspoons more – a half teaspoon of red pepper, and one teaspoon of black pepper. But it wouldn't

84

keep too good in warm weather.

ৰ

It was my job to make the scrapple. I'll tell you what I put in there, but maybe you don't want to know. I boiled the hog's head and the liver and all the scraps. I boiled the liver separate, and that water I would throw away, but all the rest was saved. I picked all the meat off the head and them other bones and chopped it all up with the liver. Then I mixed it back with some of the broth I saved, and I cooked that on the stove. After that I poured it all in a pan and let it harden up a little.

The scrapple you get now ain't nothing. I used to like it fried with a couple of eggs in the morning. I would go out to the smokehouse and get a pan, cut the mold off, and fry it up. If a kid sees a piece of mold nowadays they take a fit. Mold won't kill you; it's what penicillin's made of.

ৰ

They butchered some big hogs, but I think about two hundred pounds is the best size. You raise 'em up to two hundred pounds and you got a good hog, some good meat. It takes, oh, about four months old to get him there. You got to keep him chewing though. If he stops chewing, then he's done. You almost got to wake him up at night to keep him chewing. You change up foods on him about three or four times a week, and you give him something in between there that he'll just go and get crazy about. Yes sir, if you want good hog meat, you got to keep him chewing.

■

Timber

*"There was a sawmill stuck
in every woods."*

I worked in the lumber mills when I was a youngster.
I worked in Griffiths Neck and Hurleys Neck and in Tripps
Neck too. It was a great thing. Sawmills was the only
employment there was. You worked in a sawmill or you
didn't have no job. All of that land was big pine timber
then, great old timber, thousands of acres of it, and it was
sawmills everywhere. There ain't nothing but bushes now.
I hauled timber with oxen and with mules. I drove both
for years. I done it all: ran the big saw, fired the boilers
for the steam, worked the log carriage. I done everything
what they done in a mill.

಄

Used to be a lot of big old pines around. You still find
great old stumps on some of them creeks in the marsh.
There's a place down on Griffith Neck they called Vessel
Point when I was a boy; had trees on it as big as molasses
barrels. It was old-growth pine and a world of it. People
came there and made log canoes. Last time I was down,
I could still see the skids where they took logs out to
the creek. They cut logs and made canoes right there. It
took one log for the bottom and two for the sides. If you
wanted a big canoe, it would be four for the sides. They
would make the keel and level it out, then put them long
bolts through and bolt it all together. Then they'd take
an adz and shape her up. They'd slide it to the creek, put
up the mast, and go on out the creek with her. They did

that till the trees was all gone. Everybody used log canoes on the bay in them days.

୨ଈ

They had a big sawmill down there where the boat ramp is in town, and there was a big lumber yard there. Jim Higgins owned it. The whole block there was a big flour mill and a big lumber mill clear up to Middle Street. Old man Higgins built the houses there on Middle Street, corner of Race and Middle. Those houses were new houses when I was big enough to remember them. I would say they was probably built in 1900.

He had a steam mill, and the same engine that run the saw mill run the flour mill. It was a big one, and they had another engine that run on coal oil. It was some kind of a combustion engine.

They used the river to float the logs there. They'd cut the logs beside the river and put 'em overboard, and they'd put 'em together in a raft. They put a pole across 'em, and what they done: they had horseshoes — old horseshoes — and they'd sharpen the points of 'em and drive 'em down on the pole to hold the logs together. They'd make that raft and pull it up on the flood tide. Then they'd pull the horseshoes out so they wouldn't tear up the saws.

୨ଈ

I'll never forget when that mill burned down. There was no fire engines in Vienna then, not like you have today. It come a northwest wind, and it froze. The fire started in the mill and burned down a store and some houses up from the river. And from way up where the fire started, a piece blowed all the way down to that first farm on the Elliotts Island Road, and it caught up there on the shingles. Most of the houses had them dry wood shingles then. It like to burn up the world that night. They poured water and done what they could. They called Salisbury, and they sent a fire

87

engine over here on a train.

We went out in the yard over in Indiantown, and, God, you could pick up a pin in that yard. There was light everywhere. I wanted to go down there, but we had no way to go. We stood in that gale wind – it must of been zero. That was in the twenties.

❧

My father was in the lumber business when I was just a small kid. I was born in 1896. He always preferred cutting piling to lumber, because there was nothing like the expense of getting piling out and rafting it to Baltimore that it was to bring logs to the sawmill and cut them up into boards. He only ran the mill when he didn't have orders for piling.

The people he sold to in Baltimore would give him orders way ahead, sometimes in the fall when it was too late to raft. You couldn't send them up after the stormy weather would come; it was too risky. Sometimes he would have orders for thousands of piling to deliver the next year. Usually the starting of the rafts up the bay would happen in April. They rafted earlier, but usually the tugboat didn't go before the 15th of April.

Those pilings were cut all over the lower portion of Dorchester County from Crab Point to Taylor's Island. A lot of them were cut on Taylor's Island. The logs were put in strings, or tows as they called them, and carried through the creeks because you could only get the width of one section of piling through the spans of the bridge. They had to be made up in a raft after they got through the bridge.

You did more than just nail a pole across to hold the rafts. We used chains, chains with toggles, and wedges or dogs with rings into them, and sharpened horseshoes to drive in and hold the chains. And you bored holes in the butt of every outside log to put the chains and toggles through. It was a complicated rig when you had to tow more than a thousand piling. And there were cross-logs, two that went on the head section all the way across so the tugboat could tow by that. When that thing got out on the bay, it was a lot of weight; and if the old tugboat got into a little wind, the harder the tugboat pulled it, instead of coming up and planing like a workboat, it would go down. You'd have to slack up a little or the whole thing would go under.

On the cross-logs you had to have lamp posts. You'd take a three or four-inch pole and fasten it to the cross-log with horseshoes. There had to be two on the head, two on the tail, and one in the middle. There had to be five lanterns, coal oil lanterns, and they had to be lit when you were moving at night. Sometimes when you got in a squall, the water was up on those lamp posts almost to the bottom of the lantern. The raft would go down under the water five or six feet.

In those days there were horses all over the city; horses were used for everything then. They were used for deliveries, for riding, and one time even to pull the streetcars in Baltimore. There were no automobiles. My father used to buy old horseshoes by the barrel. I've gone in the wagon or in the boat to the old steamship wharf at Taylor's Island and Wingate Point, Little Hooper's Island, and got barrels of horseshoes from the blacksmiths' shops in Baltimore. The local blacksmith would sharpen them and fix them up so you could drive them. Most of them had a little tab on the end, and he had to heat that and beat it out. We drove the horseshoes over the chain on the rafts. It would cost less for the country blacksmith to fix those up than the Baltimore blacksmith. They were sent down in the rough, just like they were taken off the horses' feet. Blacksmiths then were – the old saying is: there was one in every corner of the fence almost.

We used ox teams to get the pilings out to the nearest water that you could float them in. The ox teams were so slow that you always tried to haul them to a landing somewhere on some creek or ditch. Why, we even dug some places, and you had to do that all by hand with just a shovel or spade. You didn't have the draglines like you do nowadays. But it would still save so much time. The oxen were mighty good in the woods, but they were so slow you had to shorten your distance every way you could.

I can remember in Baltimore City there was the J. S. Hoskin's Lumber Company that my father sold thousands of pilings to. When they got them, they sold them to the pile-driving people and contractors who built wharves. And there was another company he sold a lot to: That was H. L. Gruve.

In those days there was no creosote, no treatment for piling or lumber. The steamboat wharves – they were everywhere – and the diking and private wharves were built out of oak pilings, and the oak pilings all had to be carried to Baltimore by sailing schooners.

My father had his own schooner. Her name when he bought her was the Alexander McCullough. He had to rebuild her, and when he rebuilt her, he renamed her the L. T. Spicer. She's still in the river over there by the old homeplace.

After they were prepared, we had to put those oak pilings on top of a big scow. He had two or three scows, and you'd roll those piling on by hand until you loaded her down as deep as you wanted – was safe – and carried them down and put them on board the sailboat. The biggest scow he had was forty-five feet long and sixteen or eighteen feet wide, and it was about three and a half feet deep. We used them to haul tomatoes, cordwood, lumber, piling, and oyster shells – all kinds of things. She was cut up on either end – either end was a bow.

When they loaded the schooner, they piled those pilings on the deck, and the deck had to be shored up with something. In those days everybody cut cordwood – everybody that had a piece of woods – and sent it to Baltimore because they used it to heat their houses, heat the hotels, and fire the furnaces in a lot of factories. So they put cordwood in there to shore up the deck beams. They used to pile the piling up on the deck of that schooner to very close to as high as the door – seven feet. They had stanchions they put up with cable across it to hold them. Had to raise the booms up above that so they could shift across to either side.

They haven't used oak pilings since creosote came in. The creosote lasts so much longer. The saltwater worm, the same worm that gets into the bottom of your boat if you don't pull her up often enough, he bores into the piling. He won't cross a seam, and as long as the bark stays on an oak piling, and he couldn't get to one of the places where the limbs were cut off or the bark was skinned, he wouldn't bother it. But when he once got into it and started boring, it would be just like a honeycomb almost.

My father started in a very small way because he was a very poor man. He bought some land and cut piling first. The first sawmill he ever bought, he bought from L. W. Dudley over in Salisbury. Sawmills in those days were run by great big steam boilers. To fire up those boilers and give them steam to pull the machines in the mill, they fed them sawdust, shavings, and all those kinds of things. He cut lumber for many a boat built on Hooper's Island and in Cambridge.

I drove oxen many times. When you hauled cordwood to the landing, or in later years to where you could get to it with a saw rig, the oxcarts had a straight axle. But for hauling logs you had to use an axle with an arch to it. Those carts run anywhere from five, five and a half to eight foot in height. My father had two eight-foot carts. Those old, big carts used to take three yoke of oxen to pull them. As I said before, they were slow, but they were much better than horses or mules. They were more careful and were not as excitable. Their feet were big and kind of spread out, and they didn't mire down when the woods was wet.

Sometimes you hauled just one big log, but if you were

hauling smaller logs, you would pile a whole bunch of them together, get the cart over it, and swing them up. You had to learn how to spread the weight right. You were supposed to have a little weight on their necks to make it easier for them to pull it. You backed over the log and dropped your hooks down on it. We used grab hooks. You would buckle the front end up with a buckling chain so it wouldn't catch in things. You would hook your swinging chain a little past the middle of the log so there was more weight in the front, so to give the oxen some weight on their necks. You would swing it up till you got it into the arch of the axle, then you would throw your buckling chain under there and pull it up. If the oxen were broken right, when you got the log up under there, you would smack them on the back and the head and say, "Down," and they'd hold their heads down so you could buckle your chain. Then, when they raised their heads up, the log would come off the ground.

There were old landings all around the place where people would take their oxcarts and haul cordwood down to these landings. I could still take you up and down these old creeks and see the old poles where they used to have the landings, poles with dirt on top of them to make it solid, sticking out in the creek. It's washed now and left the old poles. They poled the scows down with the tide. When the tide turned, you fastened it to the bank and waited for the next tide. You loaded and unloaded them by hand, by block and fall. I used to have blisters on my hands as big as I don't know what.

ॐ

I thought I was the only man around anymore that could put a yolk of oxen to a cart and go get a load of logs. I drove an oxcart for years. I made enough money doing that to buy an automobile. The first new car I ever had cost me three hundred and twenty-five dollars. I got about a dollar and a half or two dollars a day according to how things were, and

I saved up for that car.

They were Herefords I had. They were white-faced, red with a white face, and they were as big and strong and mean as anything you seen in your life. Run away every day. Run away every day, they would.

I hauled piling down to the wharf where they had a canning house. There's nothing left there now but the old piling. I hauled them out of the swamp – that whole wharf of piling – one at a time. One day I come out of that swamp and hand-steered left, hit way ahead of the tree, and that off-steered the one on the other side. That ox reared up and bellered and ripped as hard as he could rip and turned the cart over on one wheel. And the piling, of course, come down across the hand-steer, the left one, come right across his head. His eyes popped out, and he was choking, and that off-steer was jumping up and down and all around. I grabbed the ax out of the cart and come back and hit him right in front of the eyes with that ax and knocked him on his knees. Then, when he got up, he was quiet. If he was going to kill the hand-steer by choking him to death, I just as soon kill both of 'em as have one. I hit him right in the middle of the forehead with that ax, and he behaved hisself after that.

I had to punch the bows out of the hand-steer and tee him up so I could get the piling off his head. I rolled the piling off his head and let him get up. He was almost choked to death. His tongue was hanging out, and his eyes was popping, but I got him back to the cart. I got 'em yoked up to the cart again. Then I had to loosen the cart and carry 'em back and hook 'em to the wheel. I had to pull her back on her feet, hook 'em up to the cart again, and come on out. I was sixteen or seventeen years old.

I worked them oxen every day for about three years, and they run away every day as long as they lived. Oh, but they were powerful. Man, they could just pull up a heavy load.

When them oxen would run away, I'd sit on the front of

93

that cart and hold on. When they got a little bit tired and started slowing down, then I'd get cracking with that whip, run 'em till their tongues hung out, trying to break 'em from running. Get that blacksnake whip and wrap 'em up, wrap 'em up. It never done a bit of good.

I learned to drive oxen when I was a little boy. My father had a pair of calves and had me a cart made, four wheels with a tongue. He made a little yolk and put it on them calves. They weren't much higher than a dog. I'd get up there and drive 'em all around the field. Them calves learned me how to drive oxen when I was seven years old.

ða

Old Ed that worked for Arthur – he's dead now – I can just see him walking to work with his whip over his shoulder, a great big whip. He was six-foot two or three and real heavy. He could cut a fly off a hoss or an ox and never touch the ox.

Arthur bought a pair of hosses – I'll never forget 'em – one brown and one black – Betty and Moxie. They were green-broke, just like a green-broke puppy. He got 'em to work in the woods. I remember him tell Ed: "I don't want you to hurt 'em, but I want you to teach 'em something."

I can hear old Ed, "Yas sir." He never talked much, just "yas sir," and "no sir."

He went down in that swamp with that pair of hosses, and it sounded just like somebody in there with a automatic .22. Lord a-mighty! "Kapow! Kapow! Kapow!"

When he got out of there with that load of logs, I don't believe them hosses' bellies were a foot off the ground. Damn, they were pulling, and they were lathered up. Every here and there you'd see a little ruffled place across their ass where he cut 'em a little bit. He just ruffled the hair a little bit. He could talk to 'em.

ða

I was in the wood business once. I'd cut and saw it up and haul it to Cambridge for six dollars a cord. They sold the old-growth timber out of the swamp, and I cut firewood after that in there. I pulled it out with horses, them old, big-footed horses.

Moore used to cut timber back there too. He had a little pair of mules and a timber cart. He'd go out there with a crosscut saw and saw that old tree down. He'd square it under this old timber cart and haul her up to the mill.

I got him to clean up when they dug this ditch through here. Them old mules he had really tickled me. He'd drive 'em up in there, and he'd want to turn around. Where they cut those limbs and brush, it was all piled up. Them little mules would rear up on that brush and come down. It beat anything I ever seen. He'd talk to 'em. Sometimes he'd use the reigns a little, and they'd rear up and come down on that brush. He was hot with 'em. Them was a right nice pair of little mules he had.

There were some big trees back there in them days, all that old growth. When they got ready to build this church up here, they went around and people donated a tree or something. I told Wilmer, "You go down and get the biggest pine you can find, carry it up to the sawmill, and saw it into lumber for that church." It's the church right up here.

It was Short who cut my timber out here. He'd cut 'em five or six foot, skin 'em and rank 'em up to dry. I would haul it to the mill.

One night, man, I like to fall out. I couldn't get the truck in the swamp. I don't know how many cord he had cut in there, but it was a mess of it. I was back there with the old mule and the horse cart, and damn, everything turned right black. It was hot. It was in the summertime anyway. I said, "I believe I'm a goner this time." So I sat down and rested for a while, and I slowed up and got it all loaded. I hauled it down there the next day.

&

95

There was a sawmill stuck in every woods nearabout. They didn't haul logs to one place like they do now. They cut the log and took it a little ways to a saw. They used a ox team or mule or horse team – whatever they had – to drag it under a timber cart. You move more in one truck load today than they sawed in a month. Peckerwood mills. That's what they called 'em: "Peckerwood." That's where the wood-pecker come in. They used to make as much sawdust in a day as a woodpecker could make.

᠊᠊

Cutting timber has killed many a one in these parts. It's easy enough to do. They fall the wrong way; a limb breaks off; they hit another tree and a piece breaks off and throws back on you. That man over to Secretary – it popped his eyes right out of his head.

᠊᠊

I cut this big old pine tree and walked off to the side watching it go. Next thing I know, I was picking my butt off the ground. Old dead tree behind it broke off. I never seen it and never heard it. Hit me right on top of the head. She struck me so hard she busted the whole front right out of my drawers.

᠊᠊

It's a dangerous job in these sawmills. One got killed down here at Linkwood. They just got a new saw, and they were setting it up. It snatched him in there and cut his head right off. Seems like somebody else got killed in there too. There's two others got killed right around here. It was some logs rolled on one of 'em.

᠊᠊

When I was a kid, they brought some logs down to the station, great big old logs. I guess they was to patch the bridge. And them logs come off that flatbed and caught an old man and knocked him down, and they rolled over him and killed him dead as a hammer. We run on down there from school. They had the old man covered up, and we didn't get to see him, but we seen the print of him laying there.

They run a railroad track from up in the woods clear out to Honga River. The old track's still there. It was Bell Lumber and Honga River Lumber. They had sawmills in Golden Hill. They hauled logs on that railroad, and one boy got killed on there. He was an evil man. They say he had a goose one time that wouldn't set on her eggs. He cut her legs off and said, "Goddamn, you'll set there now." He was mean. He killed a hobo. The hobo was leaning up against a chimney getting warm. The old man heard a noise and went out there and killed him with a shotgun. You could kill hobos then. Nobody would say nothing. This was the same old man got killed down there in the woods. They told him, "You better not stand so close to the railroad track when them cars come by. One of them logs might fall off and kill you." Before that day was over, one come off there and killed him. They carried him home in a horse cart, and his wife said, "Don't bring him in here and put him in my clean bed."

More Industry, Jobs & Crafts

"He wouldn't take a job biting holes in donuts."

Used to be a lot of people lived in the necks. Lands o' mercy! In Hurley's Neck they lived from the lake clean up to Crossroads. A lot of 'em muskratted; a lot was watermens. They done this, that, and whatnot to make a living. My granduncle and my grandfather were great oystermen when they were young men. They planted oysters and they raised oysters. They had a sailboat called the Agnot. She was a sloop. They hauled oysters to Baltimore and Seaford and every place on that sailboat. But all that was before I was born, back in the 1800's.

❧

You could always find something to do if you wanted to work when I was a kid. I made myself a little timber cart one time. I had this bird dog, and I made a harness for him. I'd huckster for Pop. He would stick a net out in the creek and get perch and stuff, and I would huckster 'em around Mardela. I'd go to somebody's house and say, "Lay down! Stay!" and that dog would lay down right to the cart. I'd come back: "Come on," and we'd go on to the next house. We had the fish bunched up – a quarter a bunch I think it was – six or seven perch on there.

❧

We had a way to make money before Christmas when I lived at the old farm: We used to make wreathes. You go out in the woods and gather the stuff: holly and grapevines and crowsfoot. You'd take a turn of grapevine and wire it together. Then you'd wire the crowsfoot on there and the holly – mostly it was crowsfoot. Mom and everybody would stay up nights and make 'em. It was easy money. We carried 'em over to Fruitland. They had an auction over there. They would line up at that auction, buy them wreathes up, and ship 'em to the cities. You sold 'em by the dozen. I forget now what we got for 'em.

ॐ

There was a lot of industry around one time, more than today. They used to have a lot of stave mills around here to make staves for barrels and nail kegs. The staves were rounded out, and you'd see 'em crossed up and stacked all out there in the sun to dry. They had a canning house or two in every town, and they had shirt factories and basket factories and mills – saw mills and flour mills. They were stuck every place there was. A man even had a button factory down below here. I think sometimes he might still make buttons there, but I guess he don't hire nobody anymore.

ॐ

I worked one time down in Griffith Neck, in that swamp back next to the marsh. They had a railroad back in there. It was small with little, dinky carts. I'd haul logs up to the railroad with a ox. It was the only way you could get back in there. God! All that water! I was trying to get a job for ten cents a hour in the sawmill down at Ralph's, in the heading mill. They made nail-keg heads in there at that time. There was a lumber yard there and a mill. It was continuous through that sawmill. The logs went through the saws, through the kiln, through the heading mill, and right out onto a railroad car. They kept it moving, one carload coming, and one carload going out. That's just the way it was every day and every night. They just made the heads and the bottoms here. The staves they made in Virginia at that time. They had three or four stave mills there.

Sawing staves was a dangerous business. I saw a colored fellow in Wakefield, Virginia one time, and I watched him sawing staves. He didn't have neither finger, all of 'em short or gone. Every finger was half, two-thirds, or all of it gone. He had to use the heel of his hand. He'd sawed staves for so many years he had no fingers left.

There was another old man there. He used to brag: "I've sawed in a stave mill for nine years, and look at my fingers; I've still got 'em all." That was pretty remarkable. You can go around a stave mill and hardly find a person who got all his fingers.

When I started there at the mill, they had nobody to work the mechanical end. The boss said, "I'll give you thirty-five dollars a week. That's more than I can afford to pay, but I'm gonna give it to you because I want you." That's the first time I ever was hired by the week, and I didn't realize that a week was seven days and seven nights. I was a mechanic, a truck driver, and a jack-of-all-trades. I worked all the time, just about. I hardly ever got any sleep. I was boss in the woods, was in charge of the trucks, and I drove one of 'em part-time. Half the time I'd work all day long and then take a load up to Pittsburgh at night, unload it, come back, and go to work again. I don't remember what the speed limit was then, but I remember how fast my truck would go: twenty-eight miles an hour loaded. She had the throttle on the dash. I used to pull it all the way back, take my feet off, and set there all night long. She never got to twenty-nine while I drove her. I left here at five o'clock in the evening, and I'd run till I got to Pittsburgh. I was supposed to be there at eight in the morning. All night, and never stopped except to pay the fare on the tollway.

We had one of the first gasoline saws down there ever was made. Henry Disten made it. They used to make cross-cut saws, and then they made this gasoline power saw. We got it down there in '42 or '43. Man, it was about three feet long, and it was so heavy it took two men to lift it, one on either end. It was a crude thing. I'll bet it weighed seventy-five or eighty pounds, but it would saw them trees down. It might of been the first chain saw ever made. It was the first one we ever seen around this neck of the woods.

I was still working there when they broke it up, and another fellow and I moved the mill to Virginia. We worked all summer moving that plant. They wanted me to go with 'em, but I wouldn't go.

೫

It was a big fire when that mill burned down. It was a stave mill and a lumber mill in there, and I don't know what all. It was a big place down there. They had two old boilers all bricked up for steam to run it with. I was up – Pop was with me – to Newark, New Jersey with a load of watermelons. We were coming in – it was three or four in the morning – and we kept seeing this fire. Man, the whole sky was red. When we got home, everybody was up watching it.

೫

I was getting fifty cents a day working on the farm. My brother was working in a canning house, and he got seventy-five cents. In 1918 he got the flu. It killed up nearly everybody that year. Every house had somebody dead, and sometimes all of 'em in one place. My brother's boss lived right beside us. He wanted me to come to work in my brother's place, so I went. The job I had was putting juice in the cans with tomatoes. There was a bucket of water setting there, and I had a little cup. I poured a little bit in every can to fill it up.

The boss said, "Now, by golly, you see some strange man come in here, you go and hide, 'cause you're under age."

So that's what I done. When I seen that man coming, I got out of there.

I started to haul tomatoes when I was nowhere near old enough to drive a truck. I couldn't have been over twelve or thirteen years old. Drive that old Ford truck down there and get in that line with all them other truck drivers – I thought that was something. That lasted about two trips. I pulled up there as big as Billy-Be-Damned. Baker said, "Come over here." He put me to work shooting cans or shooting cases, toting skin buckets.

The labor man would come now and then. All them canning houses were right on the edge of the woods, and kids would run everywhere. God a-mighty!

❧

There were a lot of canning houses around here one time. They used to build 'em on a river or a creek, a place to throw all the tomato skins and everything else. It was the same way down to Drawbridge. Man! We used to go down there and catch the biggest old carps. The carps loved that stuff.

❧

There were two canneries along the river when I was a boy. They dumped the skins overboard and let them go down the river. Both canned tomatoes; that was the big thing. Everybody growed tomatoes. You'd get ten cents for a five-eighths basket, and that was big money. If there was a big crop that year, maybe they'd go down to eight cents. They paid two cents a basket to get them picked. I picked many a basket for two cents.

❧

Lewis Wharf was an old business already when I was just a boy. I guess it was there from the first people on the river. It was a lot of business went through that place: clip-

102

per ships and then the steamboats.

My grandfather supplied honey for the steamboats. He had a hundred and fifty hives one time. People would run back and forth on the steamboats, and they'd eat on there and even sleep on there. They always wanted honey. He sold them a lard can full of honey just about every day.

The boat came every other day, one day going to Baltimore and one day coming back. One boat was the Avalon. I can't think of the rest.

ᴥ

Everything came and went on the steamboat one time. The steamboat stopped at Lewis Wharf every time, coming and going, and at the custom house in Vienna. If you had a pig or a hog or a calf and you wanted to sell it, you put it on the steamboat and sent it to Baltimore. They had a pen in the bottom of the old custom house to put the animals until the boat came for them. I've seen four or five calves and maybe three or four pigs in there, and chickens. Of course the old custom house was there when the ships would stop here from England and everywhere. That's been there, I guess, two hundred and fifty years.

There was a mill on the water right up from there that was run by a diesel engine. It was the first one around here anybody ever seen.

My father used to carry his corn and wheat to Little Brick Mill. He'd carry it and didn't wait for the grinding. He'd just trade it for some already ground. Father liked the Brick Mill. He done a good job. If the water got too low, he had a steam engine. It wasn't a big water wheel – well, it might of been ten feet. Whenever the water got low, he just hooked up a belt to the steam engine and kept going.

ᴥ

When I was a boy – oh my! When I was a young fellow, there was a mess of business in town. My lands of mercy!

There were two blacksmith shops – big blacksmith shops – two or three men into each one. And there used to be a big store that made harnesses and collars, and it had a great big old sewing machine. They could sew traces and reins and everything. You could buy leather by the whole side, tanned leather. They had a big business there. And there was a big hardware store across from a grocery. They sold plows and cultivators, and upstairs they had carriages and surreys and harnesses and things like that. There was a runway down the back. There was a ramp built way out upstairs, and then you came down the runway. On the bottom floor he had hog wire and all the housewares. You could go there and buy wagons and collars and hames and traces and harnesses and everything. There were other stores too, and a post office and an undertaker's establishment. They had caskets there and anything you'd want for a funeral. In the back they had a stable with two black horses in it, and those horses drew the hearse. They buried both my grandfathers.

ک

Back in the twenties, a blacksmith would come right to the farm. He'd come around every so often. He'd try to get a bunch together that needed him so he could make a few dollars, you know. We didn't put shoes on the field horses unless his hoof got all split; then you'd put one on to keep him from going lame. He just trimmed the work horses. But we put shoes on the riding horses and them you would put to the carriage, them what went on the road. And he'd make rims for wagon wheels and springs and whatever you needed. He could take a piece of iron and make anything out of it. I think we paid a dollar then to have him make a shoe and put it on.

ک

I was the first man ever had a hacksaw around here.

I paid thirty-five cents for it: a quarter for the saw and ten cents for the blade. People burnt wood in them days; they didn't have no coal or coal oil or anything like that. Everybody had wood saws, and the igniter on the wood saw would burn the points up, and there were no place around except Salisbury to buy points.

You couldn't hardly get to Salisbury in them days. You couldn't get across the river. They had the ferry, but the way that road was, no automobile couldn't get across there. You couldn't hardly get across the marsh with oxen and a cart. They'd be horses stuck up to their chest in there. I seen water up to the horse's belly in there with only a halfway tide. You could go by way of Sharptown and Laurel, Delaware, but you'd be gone all day driving ten miles an hour.

With my hacksaw I'd take a six-penny nail, saw the head off, stick it in the igniter, and start her up. I'd make my own points like that. One day old man Hurley saw me start to saw a nail in two. He grabbed my hand and said, "Boy, what's the matter with you; are you crazy? A saw won't saw iron."

I said, "This one will."

"Aw," he said, "you're fooling with me."

I sawed that nail in two, and he just shook his head. He couldn't understand. He never seen a hacksaw before in his life, and I was the only one had a hacksaw then. I sawed many a nail to stick in the igniters. People would cut twenty-five or thirty cord of wood, and I'd have to do it over again, but there wasn't nobody else would fool with it. It was a good business for me. I was about fifteen years old then.

❧

It come a time when we had a lot of factories, mostly little ones. Almost every town had a shirt factory. Hebron had a shirt factory. Mardela had two. Brookview had a great big one there. Sharptown had one or two, and they had a big basket factory. When that basket factory burned down, it was a big fire that night. I could see it right straight in front of this door. Sharptown had a lot of business. Shipbuilding was big there once. Ain't nothing there now but an old pickle house.

ઠ

My uncle was the greatest with woodwork you ever seen. He could make anything in the world out of wood. He was a woodworking man. He made ox whips, them blacksnake whips. He made them in the middle of the night and sell them for a dollar and a quarter apiece. Old fellow had a store up here, and my uncle bought leather from him by the side. Then he's split it open and come down to, you know, make three corners. He done the same way with the plaiting on the end. He started with the round plaiting and come down two strands. He made the staffs out of white oak. He could look at an oak tree: "Uh huh, that one will work." I seen him do it many a time. He could tell whether it would be straight-grained or not. It had to be straight-grained so the butt was true, and then he could split it out and taper it down, all the way down. When you got out there to the end, you'd have nothing. The white oak has to come out of the swamp. You can't go up on high ground and get it. You got to know what you're looking for. Then he'd take the three-sided leather and plait that around there. Then he'd put the round cracker and the two-strand on, and you had a blacksnake whip. The whole thing was six, seven feet long.

My uncle used to make a lot of stuff for wagons: wheels, spokes, hounds, hubs, tongues, stuff like that. And he made ox yokes and bows too. Then, nights, he would make the blacksnake whips. I reckon he made a thousand of them.

ઠ

I don't even make a dollar an hour sometimes, but I

was never much for setting in the house. I never did like to set in the house. I like to be out. I'm an outdoor man. When I was a young man, I didn't stay in the house none, just while I slept four or five hours. Every morning, fall of the year and winter and spring, I was up three o'clock or three-thirty, and I was in the marsh before day ever broke. I can't stay in the house. I just can't look at four walls all day, day after day. When I have to do that, I'm gone. It'll be the end of me.

ঙ

These guys lazy around the service station every day saying, "I ain't got nothing to do. I ain't got no work."

I say, "You don't want nothing to do." I've always said if a man wants something to do, he can find something to do. He might not make a big salary, but he can find something to do. You see that little paper last week: six pages of jobs, and they can't find nothing to do. I listened to this one fella the other day – why he wouldn't take a job biting holes in donuts. He wouldn't do that.

■

Hunting, Fishing & Trapping

"The ones that were good never got caught."

There weren't no geese when I was a boy. The first goose I ever seen – Old man Luther Langford had a store down here. He had a son about seventeen, and Atlee was a hunter. He hunted all his life; he hunted everything in this world. It was him what killed the goose. He brought it up there to the store and put him on the counter, turned him bottom up, and everybody went down to see that wild goose. I was ten or twelve at the time, and my father took me down to see it. Then, a few years later, we had 'em everywhere.

Atlee was a great duck hunter, and most every day he'd be shooting ducks in my father's marsh. My father would run him out, and the next day he'd be back in there. My father would say, "I'm gonna have you arrested." Of course he wasn't going to, just made like he was. The next day Atlee'd be back in there shooting again.

❧

I don't hunt no more. I used to miss it, but I don't think much about it now, not at my age. I done a lot of hunting and trapping when I was a young man; it's the way I made my living. For fifteen or twenty years I went ducking almost every day I could, and when the wind was northwest, I went on Sunday too. On a south wind they could hear me shoot, but they couldn't when the wind was northwest. I killed many a duck in my life. Not saying it to brag, but one time I was a pretty good shot. I've shot ducks as high as three weeks at a time and never missed a shot; shoot maybe twenty-five or thirty times a day and kill every one, week after week. I had one bad day, and I'll never forget that. I went down to a place called Deep Cut. I went in there, and ducks was flying everywhere, just as thick as blackbirds in a cornfield. I had forty-five shells in my coat pocket and shot every one. Picked up seventeen ducks. Took three shells to hit one. There were ducks flying everywhere, and I was missing two out of three. I couldn't shoot that day to save my soul.

ઢ

Albanus was a market hunter. He almost got sent away one time. He was talking one night about all the different things they used. He said they went skiffing one time and took a bow gun, you know, one of those big-bore guns they strapped in the bow of the boat. They would put anything in there: nails, iron, anything but glass. He said he put a hundred foot of trap chain in his gun one time. He said he shot that thing, and the chain went out there and cut the heads clean off a hundred ducks.

He was the one during Hurricane Hazel – he said he was walking by the fireplace, and the wind blew so damn hard it caused a draft and sucked him right up the chimney. He said he climbed out on the ridgepole, and just about that time one of his sons came around the corner of the house. The boy yelled, "Mom, get the gun. There's a burglar on the roof."

Albanus said, "No honey, it's just your daddy."

ઢ

The bow gun was like a little cannon, about three feet. You'd put nails, stones, and everything else in there. It was strapped in the front of the boat. One of the last ones I know they fired down here: they put it in a skiff, loaded it up, and blowed the end out of the skiff. The man like to drown out there in that creek.

109

The punt gun was a long rifle. They were as long as the boat or longer, and they were muzzle loaders. All them guns you mounted on the boat shot black powder, and you would load 'em with what you had.

But the boys that shot for money didn't use that stuff. They used regular automatics or pumps, and they welded extension tubes under 'em to hold ten shots. They shot for the market. On a real ca'm night you could hear it out on the river. You could hear geese honking. First thing you know, you hear "boom! boom! boom!" A lot of boys used them old lights up in the bow with the big reflector, and they shot out of a skiff. The ones that were good never got caught.

&

I learned to shoot ducks from my uncle. I thought that was the greatest thing in the world. He trapped ducks; had a little branch come up there behind his barn, and he had his trap setting in there. He'd throw a little bit of corn in that trap, and the next morning there'd be anywhere six, seven, or eight ducks in there.

I had a little, single-barrel gun – paid three dollars and a quarter for it – and I'd be over to his place before light. He'd be setting back at his big old stove – a Home Comfort Stove. It was a cook stove. He'd have a piece of seasoned oak in there, and he'd be setting back with his feet shoved in that oven clean up to his knees – every morning. I can see him do it now: his old pipe in his mouth and his mustache and whiskers. After a while he'd say, "Well, we'll go down and get 'em out."

He'd turn 'em out one at a time, and I'd start shooting. At first I missed about half of 'em, but after a while I got to where I'd get pretty near every one. He'd take his toe and lift the gate up, and they'd come out flopping and beating and quacking. That's the way I learned to shoot ducks. I couldn't wait to get down there and shoot them ducks. I was up in the middle of the night. I was crazy about that.

I used to be a great hunter – thought I was. I'd be in the marsh before it got light, decoys out and everything ready to shoot some ducks. I shot ducks for a living, shot 'em and sold 'em. It was against the law, but I shot 'em and sold 'em just the same. That's what I done for fifteen years. I'd put 'em in the back end of the barbershop, and a man from Salisbury come and get 'em sometime in the night. He always wanted a male and female tied together. I'd put 'em in the back room under the floor in a leaf bed, and down in the floor there was this old cigar box. The next morning my money would be in that box. I sold ducks to him for fifteen years and never saw him but once, and then I wasn't closer than fifty yards. He was a white man. I had no idea what his name was. I sold him thousands and thousands of ducks – a dollar and a quarter for two. It was good money. It was a good living. Anywhere else, ten dollars a week was all you could make. I sold him mallards and summer duck, and some were one thing and then another, but when they got on the plate, they were all black duck then. Only black duck went on the table in the restaurants.

I had three hundred and forty-two acres of marshland, and I had seven different places I baited. I could shoot one every day and would only shoot each place once a week. Sometimes I went weeks without missing a shot. One time I shot five times and killed seventeen. Another time I shot ten times and killed twenty-seven or twenty-eight.

I used a Remington Model 11. I shot her so much I wore out the barrel and all the parts. I rebuilt all the working parts into her four or five times. I shot the barrel out and had to put new barrels on her. The barrel would get as thin as a piece of paper. You could squeeze her with your fingers.

I only saw a warden but one time. I didn't realize it was a game warden until he got right up on me, but he didn't catch me. I had a skiff with a motor – an inboard motor –

and when I realized it was him, I cranked her up and got across that creek just a-flying. I went out running, went off and left him. He was in a boat with just a paddle, so he couldn't catch me. That's the only time I ever had a game warden to bother me.

ॐ

The best shot I seen in my life was old Lloyd. He never missed. He never missed! I hunted with him from about 1927 till 1944, and I never saw him miss a shot. When he shoot, it fall. But one time up on Chicone Creek – Nick and Travis was with him – they said he shot a duck and had to shoot it twice. Hit him the first time, but he didn't fall, and Lloyd had to shoot him again to get him down. Travis was in the blind with him and said Lloyd shot, and the duck started falling down. He got near about to the water and commenced to gathering himself up. Lloyd shot him again and killed him. Everybody here talked about that around the store and around the service station. "Lloyd shot twice to kill one duck!" It was something unusual. They carried on about that for a week or ten days. That was a great thing around here.

ॐ

The best ducking dog I ever seen was old Brownie. He could see a duck ten miles off. He'd sit there and perk them ears up. You could look and look, and after a while you'd see 'em coming. If a duck would go down behind the grass and Brownie not see it, I would throw a handful of mud in that direction and say, "Over there, Brownie," and he'd go and bring it back.

He was two years old when I got him and never seen no water in his life – no more than rain water. I brought him home and carried him out there on the marsh. He wouldn't even get his feet wet; come to a puddle and jump over it. I got him in the boat one day and pushed him over in the creek.

112

I would bring a duck home and throw it on the floor. He'd nuzzle it around, but he wouldn't pick it up. It took a long time to break him. I'd throw one wing, and he'd get it. Then I tied two wings together, then the wings and the feet. Finally he'd bring the whole duck. In the end he was the best dog I ever seen.

ॐ

Old man Brittingham was gunning over on Hip Roof Road one year. He said every morning that whole ducking season he stepped across this little gut. There was a stump out there in the middle of that gut, and every morning he stepped on that same stump. Gunning season wasn't over till the end of February, and it warmed up one day as it sometimes does in February. He went out there and stepped on that stump, and the son-of-a-gun walked away. It was a snapping turtle buried there in the mud all winter long. But the old man was known to lie.

ॐ

Dupont had a clubhouse on the creek down there. The boys would drive their big cars down that old pole road. It was two stories, that clubhouse, and down on the bottom of it you could drive your car in there on boards. They would stay upstairs overnight. For all the money he had, it weren't nothing elaborate. I'd carry 'em ducking some-times. Captain George Richardson used to keep his boat tied there, and he would carry 'em across the bay to Snake Island and all out there to the head of Fishing Bay.

We went in there one morning – there was four or five of us – and it was down to zero. I had an old wooden pat. We went out in that creek, busting ice every foot we went. We got down there about a mile, and that creek froze up again. We had to beat and thrash all the way back up. The old motor wouldn't half run. It was an old Water Witch. But we stayed out there; killed ducks and couldn't get to half

113

of 'em; didn't have no dogs that time. We stayed out till it was dark; got over the limit and run up close to the shore before we got to the house and pitched out the extra ducks. If there wasn't nobody around, we'd pick 'em up again. Never did see a game warden out there.

ðŸ™

I've killed a thousand of them hanners and hawks. Gilbert's mother could fix 'em the best I ever eat in my life. We'd kill a load of 'em and carry 'em down there. People quit work to shoot hanners and hawks. That used to be the thing. Some people lived on 'em.

You put up a hawk and hanner pole in a pine tree – a long pole. You'd lash it or nail it anyway you could get it up there. Then you'd hide in shotgun range. Them hawks and hanners would line up on that pole, and you could shoot and wipe the whole pole clean. In the evening you could hear shots everywhere on the island and up along the shore. You could find poles everywhere. You'd get on the shore where they come up – damn – you could melt your gun barrel off. State game wardens would never bother you much till the federal boys got so bad about it.

ðŸ™

I don't think you're supposed to shoot doves. I only went once, and I didn't want to go to start with. A bunch from over to Salisbury went out birding that morning. It was Buck and his son and another one – three head altogether – and they come in at noon and wanted me to go with them for doves. I said, "I ain't been hunting doves in my life." You ain't got nothing if you do shoot one, a bunch of feathers it looks like to me. I've found them in the woods in the wintertime. You find them, but you don't find the other birds. They can't take the cold.

But I went. It was a farm they hunted the other side of Eldorado. It was corn stalks still standing in there. We hadn't gone very far in the field before an old dove come by.

"Shoot him!" they yelled.

I didn't want to shoot, but I put up: "Pow!" And I never heard nothing holler so pitiful since I was born. He come down in circles. I think I just broke his wing.

"Go get him," they said.

I said, "Not me. I'm never go get him. He'll stay there." So one of them went and got him.

I never shot neither another one of them. I said, "Shit! Any other time I'd of missed him."

کا

I'd like to live long enough to walk every mile again that I walked coon hunting. I figure I'd never die for a long time. The biggest coon we ever killed was in the daytime, and it weighed twenty-nine pounds. We killed it in the water. Wilmer took it home and weighed it, and that's what he said anyway.

I went back here with him one night, and the dogs got on a trail. Wilmer was standing there by a maple tree. That coon come across that little field and run right up Wilmer; thought he was a tree. Now some might doubt that, but if they knew Wilmer, they'd know better. I said that beats all I ever seen. It run right up him same as it was on a tree.

We took him coon hunting in our car one time. He come on a skunk in the woods and hunted that skunk down and stomped it and killed it. He had so much stuff on him. We took his clothes off and started a fire and smoked 'em to get the smell down so we could go home. Stomped that skunk till he killed it! You can just imagine what he smelled like, and he didn't even know it. He was just that way.

They called him Abraham; looked just like Lincoln. There was one thing he didn't like was baths. He hadn't take a bath, I know, since his mother gave him one when he was a little fella. His mother may have give him one.

115

He used to live in an old house down here. I made him move out 'cause I wanted to work on that house. We found him another place, and he said, "You'll have to help me move." So I moved him. He had old rabbit dogs, all kinds, chained to the bed and everywhere. I went in there with a truck and backed up to the door. He said, "I got a dead dog here; been dead two or three days." And there it was in his bed.

When I went coon hunting with him, he had sixteen dogs – I counted them – in one room. He slept right in that room on the cot, and them run around all night with the lamp burning. He never did feed them dogs. Their insides would shine right through with the light; that's how poor they were. He called one Wolfie.

His car tags run out one time, and he didn't have no money to get new ones. He went the whole year with no tags, and nobody ever stopped him. Yeah, it's a shame you didn't know Wilmer.

I'm done my coon hunting days. I'm past that now for good.

ta.

Old Moore said he went coon hunting one night. He told me that story a dozen times if he told me once. Said he was right by hisself, and he treed this coon – his dogs did. It went right up this old gum tree. He throwed his light up there and looked all around, but he couldn't see nothing. So he climbed part way up that tree for to see better. He finally throwed his light over to another tree – a big old tree – and there he was. He looked around, and there was a grapevine went across to the other tree. He said, "If that coon can walk on that grapevine, I can too." He said he got up there and walked right across that grapevine; went right over to that other tree and got his coon.

That night while he was coming up, he said he got to thinking about it and how he could of gone down and the

116

dogs eat him up. Said it scared him so bad he had to lay down right there. He'd set and tell that stuff all night long if you'd set and listen to it.

❧

Moore treed a coon over there to Red Banks one time – he told that. He clum up this tree and couldn't get down. He said to the boys, "Take the ax and cut her down." Said those boys took the axes and went to chopping on this big old tree. He said, "Now you let me know about the time she gets ready to fall."

So they yelled, "She's going over!"

I guess he was on the right side. Hadn't, he'd of got buried in there somewhere. Said he got up, stepped right off, and went on. He'd laugh about that.

❧

I had a good coon dog. I wouldn't take nothing in the world for him. I'd follow him wherever he went. If the coon didn't go up till the morning, I went where that dog went. He was my dog. When he died, I never went no more.

❧

Just before you get to Savanna Lake, old man Long John lived there. He was a real tall man, and everybody called him Long John, and he had a boy named Lawrence. They had a little field by the house, four or five acres, where they had corn and 'maters and such. This one fall two deers come out there, a male and a female, and they were grazing behind the house. He went and got his bullet rifle – Lawrence did – and shot the buck, shot him and killed him. Everybody went down and looked at him, and nobody knew where in the world it come from. That's the first deer ever was in the county that anybody knowed of. Come to find out that old man Dupont had a hunting place down county and turned a pair of deers out. It was a male

117

and a female. They strayed away, and he didn't know what went with them, and it was them that went down to Hurleys Neck to Long John's field.

ॐ

It weren't that long ago we didn't have no deer. I never seen a deer till I was maybe – I guess I was almost thirty-five years old. I was over on the back place, back there where them old apple trees was, right there against the woods, and I seen this track in the sand. I told Howard: "Now somebody's hog must of went back there."

He said, "I imagine it might be a deer." He said, "They seen one over here to Eldorado just the other day in Willis Brinsfield's pound, a deer in there with his cows."

So from that on they kept coming, a few more every year. It was three or four year before they had a season. I didn't have nothing but a shotgun with slugs. I'd say it was another four or five year before I got one. Then it come to be they were all over. You'd go on the back place in the evening, and it seemed there'd be one back of every tree. The field would be full of 'em, and it would be a commotion in the branch every time you walked in there. One season – every time I went back there, one would stick its head out somewhere: "Payowww!" I had 'em hanging up a tree everywhere.

That's when the boys up in the city found out about it and started coming down and leasing all these farms for their clubs. It's kind of leveled off now, but there's still a mess of 'em around.

ॐ

I've brought out three dead deer hunters. I found one of 'em – I was back in a field and thought I heard someone hollering. It kept hollering and hollering. I drove around there and found a man running up the road. He said, "My God, call somebody! I need help!" He said his father had a

118

heart attack and was in the marsh, and he described where it was. He ran on down the road. I walked on back in there and walked up on him. He had bogged down up to his waist. You could see where he floundered around there. His son had taken the time to go and cut two bushes with a fork in 'em and propped him up. And he's sitting up there; he's just sitting there; he's looking straight ahead, and he's deader than shit. And he's on our property. About that time some help started coming.

My uncle said, "Well, I guess I caught him."

ی

I've seen fish in this river – good heavens! I've seen two boys go out there to a morning and come back about sundown with fish in their boat clear up to their knees. I saw two boys one time had fifty-one hundred pound boxes of rockfish in one day. But you can't catch much now. It's the bad water. The fish lives in the water, and the water's so bad the fish can't live into it.

ی

Old man Jim Bennett would go down to the river about sunup, and he'd smell: "I smell a sturgeon, boys, put the seine on." If he didn't smell no sturgeon, he wouldn't put no seine on. If he did smell 'em, he'd catch four or five that day. They would bring good money, but I don't think no sturgeon come in this river in fifty years.

ی

I went to Deals Island fishing with a crowd one time, and they all got drunk. The headboat had an old Model A engine in it. After you got up past the water line, you could shove your finger through the cracks in that boat anywhere, and the wind was northeast. I said, "Damn if this ain't something." I said, "This will be my first and my last."

We got out there – wasn't another boat anywhere. The

man carrying us was drunk too. He like to fell overboard two or three times – the boys would grab him. Neither one of 'em took their rod and reel out. One was laying on the floor of the cabin; it was the only dry place you could find. The wind was blowing and driving water through them big cracks. We went along there, and after a time he shut her off. I said, "What's the matter?"

He said, "I lost my rudder."

I said, "Damn if this ain't something. Well," I said, "I'll try to fish."

We moved up and down on them waves. We were right beside this buoy. One minute I was looking way up at that buoy, and the next minute I'd be looking way down at it. I was never so scared in my life. I told that man: "Look, how are we getting back to shore?"

He said, "I don't know."

I said, "Well, I got twenty dollars here to give to you if you carry me to shore, and then you can come back out and stay the rest of the week if you want to, and I won't care."

It got rougher and rougher out there. By and by a big boat come along, and I wavered to him. That fellow came around, and damn if he didn't tow us in. I said, "Well, this is my first, and this is my last." Damn if it wasn't something.

🔊

When I first started trapping muskrats, I found a lot of wood blocks in the marsh. They were about two feet long. I didn't know what they were, but my uncle come along, and I asked him. I said, "What are these chunks of wood?"

"They're deadfalls," he said. "People would use them before they ever had steel traps. They put the block up in a muskrat lead; held it up with two notched sticks. When the rat knocked the stick off, the block fell down on top of him."

The marsh was full of them blocks. You'd go around

with your stick, and first thing you know you'd hit one; go over yonder and hit another one. They were underneath the mud and still solid; made of old heart pine and still solid as a nut.

ॐ

When I was first trapping, a man on the other side of the road going down to Elliott used two or three hundred snares in there. He could see when he had a rat; the snare would pull it up above the grass. He didn't have to go to every one; just look across there and go to them that were sprung. He trapped snares there for three or four years. He was an elderly man. Them was the only snare traps I ever seen anybody use.

ॐ

I was in the marsh trapping one day, and it was cold, the wind blowing northwest and freezing. Water blowed against that grass, and it had balls of ice on there as big as my fist. I run my skiff up against the bank and stepped over, and I went down right up to my arms. In them days I smoked cigarettes, and I had cigarettes in my shirt pocket, and matches. The first thing I thought about when I went down was to grab them matches. I grabbed them matches, and they never got wet. I got back in that skiff and got across the creek, and I set that marsh on fire. I burned my eyebrows off, and my boots got to smoking, but I dried myself off and come on out. If my matches would of got wet, I wouldn't be here today.

And I was down in that marsh the same day the boy froze to death, a fellow I knowed well. He used to be a good pitcher. I batted against him many a time. He had traps out there on the road to Elliott. He fell in and started to walk out, and he just fell down and died; froze to death. That was a bad day to be in the marsh.

When I started out that day to come back up the creek,

it had started to freeze. I'd push my boat up on the ice with my pole, and then I'd have to go up in the bow and mash the ice down. Then I'd go back and push it up again; mash it down every foot of the way. It was sleeting and freezing. I had on a warm coat, but it was ice all the way around. My uncle was down below. He left his boat and come up beside the woods. I met him in the ditch, and we come out together. He had a mustache, and it had icicles on there as big as lead pencils, and they hung clean down below his chin. The whole side of his face was covered with ice a half inch thick. It was a rough day. I had forty-two muskrats, and he had forty-one. Them muskrats weighed about two to three pounds a piece. We each had about a hundred pounds. He said, "I'll take the odd one."

When we finally got out to the car, she wouldn't start. I raised the hood, and she was full of ice. I took some gas out of the tank and set it on fire to melt that stuff off. We come out of that marsh, oh, an hour before sundown, and when I got home, it was eleven o'clock that night. There was nobody on the road but me, and the ice on that windshield so thick I couldn't see. I had to get out and dig the ice off, get back in and go a hundred yards, get out and dig it off again. From before sundown till eleven o'clock to go ten miles.

That was a '31 Chevy I had that time. I bought it from a fella – he was having trouble with it, and I told him I could fix it. He brought her up to the shop, and I fixed her up. When he come to get her, he said, "What's the bill?"

I said, "Fifteen dollar."

He said, "Give me twenty-five and keep it."

So I did, and I run that thing eleven years.

When my second son was born, he was crippled. One of his legs run right up his back. It was a pitiful thing. There was a doctor in Johns Hopkins Hospital said, "I want that boy." He said, "If I live long enough, I'm gonna fix that leg."

My wife drove the boy to that hospital every two weeks

in that car till he was four or five years old. That doctor fixed that leg so today you can't tell it. And when he finished with it, he didn't live three months after that.

ཡ

I used to gig muskrats when I was a boy. A lot of people used two five-prong gigs, but I was never able to handle two five's. I used a seven-prong.

Them rats have a right good-sized bed in there, sometimes five or six rats to the house. Sometimes you get two or three, and two or three goes out. You can hear 'em jump down the well: "Schlump! Schlump!"

You'd try to go into the house on the windward side. I used to gig 'em on a nor'west wind. You had to watch one thing though: If you throwed that gig in on one what built his house around a stump, it was rough on the arms. Fella was gigging at night one time and throwed his gig in on a stump and broke his collar bone.

I was down beside this big old pond one afternoon, and the wind was blowing a gale nor'west. I'd been trying to gig some all day, but they wasn't in. Then I went up to another house, and there was moisture on top of the bed – little drops of water on the straw – and I knowed they was starting in. The sun was only fifteen minutes high, so I grabbed my gig and started down the side of that pond. I gigged as long as I could see, and I gigged thirty-five then between sundown and dark. I was forty miles from everywhere, and it was dark. I laid the rats on top of the houses and had to go back and find 'em, put 'em in the boat, and then come up the creek to the bridge. Lord! I never got out of there till nine o'clock that night, but I had a big turn of muskrats.

I gigged for the meat and for the hides both. It put a little hole into the hide, and the buyer would fuss a little about that, but he'd take 'em. If you hit 'em in the hip or the shoulder, he wouldn't fuss much, but if you hit 'em in the middle of the back, he'd want to throw 'em out on you.

I got forty-five and fifty-five for the hides then, forty-five cents for the brown and fifty-five cents for the black. It wasn't much money, but it was something to work at.

My uncle used to amuse me gigging muskrats. He'd creep up on a muskrat house, and when he'd get up there to the house, he'd put his gig down. He'd take his pipe out, put some tobacco in there, light it up, and then he'd smoke awhile. Then, after a time, he'd pick up his gig and come down on the house. Then he'd take his tear and tear into the house. He'd have three or four in there. I used to say, "Why in the world don't you gig the house and quit fooling?" He done that many a time.

ता

We used to have trouble with people stealing musk-rats, hunting your traps at night. Two head would take a length of string and go out a piece in the marsh – so far apart – and they'd walk. When they walked that string, it would hang on the trap pole, and they'd just walk it back to your trap.

ता

I used to set traps for hawks and owls; stick a pole in a field somewhere and put a board on top to hold a steel trap. He'd come out there and pitch on it, and you'd get him. They used to have a bounty on hawks and owls both, fifty cents or something. I had heads tacked all over the cornhouse. You had to turn in the head; I believe it was to the game warden you gave 'em. After a while you didn't get nothing for 'em, and then I stopped it.

ता

We would catch turkles sometimes when we trapped the marsh down on Hog Island. I remember an old turkle Pop caught in a trap one year. We had a little trailer setting there in the yard. He threw that old turkle in the trailer,

and I guess he been setting out there in the open a month –
six weeks maybe – and it froze hard that winter.

We got to talking there one day, and Pop says, "Why
don't you take that turkle home with you? You can sell it."

I said, "Hell, it's no use to carry him home; he's dead."

He said, "He'll come to if you give him some heat."

I said, "You think so?"

He said, "Yeah."

I said, "As long as he's been out here in the open, all
froze like that?" He was just as solid as a rock.

Well, I run that thing home and put him under the
wood heater. After a while I seen him start to moving. It
was quite a time for him to thaw through, but that son-of-
a-gun, I stepped on him there on the floor, and he walked
right on with me. I sold him to Don Bouens for a dollar or
two.

Fish will freeze in the ice too and swim away when it
thaws. I saw that later on over on Bassets Pond. We went
out there skating one time on a Sunday – a bunch of us.
There wasn't all that grass in there then, and you could
skate all around. We come to a patch where two or three
fish was frozen in there, sun perch or something. After it
thaws, they say those fish will swim right away.

❧

Pappy and I used to have a gig, what we called a turkle gig. It was a piece of iron rod, and we would prod in
the mud to hit the shell of the turkle. Then we dug him
out. In the summer you would go around these branches
in a dry spell and see where he crawled. I've got ahold of
one's tail and tried to pull him out, and you can't pull him
out. You'd think his tail would come off, but you'd not
pull him out.

❧

We used to wade for the old turkle in May. They mate

125

in May. You'd beat two pieces of wood together, and they would stick their heads up. After a thunderstorm was the best time to go. You could use hip boots or waders or just a pair of tennis shoes. You'd watch when their head come up, and they'd settle right back down. Then you'd walk to 'em and feel around with your feet, and then you reach down and pick him up.

ð·

Pop used to prys the old turkle out with a stick, or he had something made up he called a turkle hook on the end of a pole. It was bent – a big old hook. I used to go with him when I was a kid and sit in the boat. He could tell all across the marsh where there was a lump or something. He'd say, "Here's one," and then he'd prys him out.

You could catch bullfrogs with that hook too. You go through the reeds in the night, and you blind him with a light. Then you reach out under his chin and hook him.

ð·

They used to have a lot of turkle pounds down in the marsh; keep 'em in there till they could sell 'em. Sometimes they would keep 'em in the pound to fatten 'em up a little bit. It was like a bulkheaded pen on the edge of the marsh. They drove boards down just like a bulkhead. Some of 'em had wire across the top.

ð·

We had a turkle once – I don't know what he weighed. Cliff put him in an old chicken crate, and he busted the rungs out of it. He got underneath the store down there, and they never could get him out. That winter, when they got the fire going real good in the wood stove, they'd be setting in that store talking, and that turkle would come alive and pick the whole store up.

ð·

Robinson caught a sea turtle out in the bay. He got it up close to the bank after a while and hooked onto it with his truck and pulled him ashore. It took a wrecker to turn him over. They said he hollowed that turtle out with an ax and nippered oysters out of that shell the whole winter.

&

We used to catch turkles out in the field when they come up from the ditch. The terrapins would crawl out there too. You'd see them come after you get the field all plowed up. You'd see him crawling out there to lay eggs.

One day I looked out, and I seen something there in the middle of the road down by the ditch. It looked like a turkle from here; looked like a nice one. Then I seen this car turn around and park right in the road. Two of 'em got out, and one walked 'round and 'round that turkle. I guess the turkle kept turning. They made about three rounds, and I seen the one reach down. I guess he got it by the tail. I knowed he didn't get it by the head, or he'd had ahold of him yet. He got him about a foot off the road, and that turkle must of run his head out. Anyway, he drops it. They look each other over for a minute more, and then they commenced to turning 'round and 'round again. By now they had three or four cars stopped, and the whole road was blocked up. Directly, after a while, they had him in the trunk.

&

The fella that married Virgie's mother used to give the Kelly boys a nickel apiece for every terrapin they could find. He'd love them little terrapins. They'd go on my back place, and Miss Kelly would go with 'em. They searched that place from one end to the other and in the branch too. A nickel apiece for every terrapin. They'd get a mess of 'em.

■

Recreation & Entertainment

"I'll bet you never heard of Hucky-
Bucky-Booster."

A girl asked me the other day what we done for entertainment in the old days. I told her, "Nothing. There weren't no entertainment."

ॐ

Uncle Ned had a gradiphone; that's what he called it anyway. It was the first one I ever seen, and it was years before I ever saw anything else besides that. It had a roll shoved on a round piece of iron. Drop that needle down on that cylinder and it run across and played a tune. Had a great big old horn to it. The needle followed the thread all the way around till it got done. Man, that was a great thing to go over there on a Sunday morning and hear that gradiphone play three or four rolls. From the time I was six or seven till I was seventeen or eighteen, the only music I heard was when Uncle Ned played that gradiphone. It had about a dozen cylinders and was colored green, light green. I'd bet two to one that daggone gradiphone's down there in the front room now. His great-grandson lives there, and whenever I see that boy, I'm gonna ask him. Of course he's seventy years old now.

ॐ

When I was just a young boy, Jimmy Higgins had a big showplace right behind the bank. It almost filled up that lot. He used to have dances and shows, different things. Once in a while he'd have a brass band in there, drums and cornets. That was some showplace. Everybody went. I used to go up there and peep in the door and watch 'em dance. There'd be a dozen or fifteen in there cutting the mustard, and they had two, three head playing the fiddle and g'itar and 'cordion. Later on then, it caught fire and burned down.

In them days there was a great big lumber yard down there. The logs come up the river on rafts, and it was a big sawmill there too. They had all kinds of lumber, a whole world of lumber. They were always building houses or something 'cause they had excess lumber they couldn't sell. He was cutting all the time. That's the reason he built that theater over there.

&

There used to be a spring and a hotel over in Mardela. Well, the spring is still there, but the hotel is gone these many years. People would come from Washington and Baltimore and everywhere on the train, and they would go to stay at that hotel and get their spring water. They shipped jugs and bottles out of there to everywhere.

Man! The Fourth of July! They had a big yard there, and tables all out in that yard. They made ice cream, homemade ice cream. There wasn't no place in Mardela you could get ice cream then. The whole place would be full of kids. That's what it was for, I guess; and all the old people out there looking after 'em. It was just full of people. You couldn't even cross your fingers out there. And when it wouldn't be light anymore, they had spark lers they would set afire. They had a big time.

&

There's a card game called Fifty-Eight. It's a Dorchester County patent. I've traveled halfway around the world and I never found anybody but the people in Dorchester County knew how to play Fifty-Eight.

129

You bid. You can bid up to fifty-eight on your cards, but you got to get them in sequence. Everybody tries to catch your King. The King is twenty-five points. You play partners, usually the men against the women. You deal out eight cards to each, and you take those cards and bid on what you got in that hand. You're trying to get fifty-eight points. They count: Ace is one; King is twenty-five; Jack's one; Ten's one; Nine is nine; Five is five; Three is fifteen; and Two is one. The rest aren't worth anything.

Let's say you had the Ace, King, Queen, and Three of Spades. That's good for a bid. You say, "I'll bid forty." It goes to the next one, and she passes. I'm your partner. If you have a hand good enough for forty, and I don't have anything compared to that, I pass. Say it goes on to the next one, and she passes. Then you get the bid and say it's Spades.

If I want to throw all mine away and get eight more, I can do it. I would keep all my Spades and try to get more to go with you to get fifty-eight. If you bid forty and get forty, that's yours. If you get forty-two, that's yours. If you don't get what you bid, you're minus the bid you make. Only the one that takes the bid can score. It moves quick. You say what you want to play to, five hundred or two-fifty.

ex.

When I was a kid, this fellow had a great old whip. He'd go in the front yard. He had an old apple tree right off his porch, and he'd snap apples off that tree one after the other. He was good. It was good entertainment in the evening to go watch him.

ex.

I never did go to dances or to the shows when we were kids. There wasn't anything close by, and you couldn't travel very far in those days. Most of the time you were too tired nights to do anything. What I did most nights was to go down to Dan Murphey's. Old man Dan would tell stories all night and dance a jig. He was good, and he must of been eighty years old then. We'd go down in a buggy, or I'd ride my horse or the old mule.

≈

The men used to spend their time at the country store. They would swap lies and tell stories and pull pranks on each other. All the old cats would hang out there. The women and the kids had to find their fun at home. You made up little games you'd play. Girls would make up songs and play with their dolls, and there were lots of games where they would hide or play hopscotch. Boys were always getting into something: bring home snakes and frogs and all kinds of things. They had their ball games, and they were always chasing everybody around. They had a game they played with their pocketknives. They would chuck 'em up, and I forget exactly how that went. It would stick some way, and they got points for that. Marbles was another game they played.

≈

I was some size before I ever seen a movie. I only got in the movies when I went to see my cousin in town. I used to think he was big stuff when he could go in the movies on Saturday. It would cost ten cents, and you could go in the morning and stay all day if you wanted to. All them old movies was silent then, and somebody played the piano. We went to see westerns, and after the movie they would give out prizes before you went home.

≈

Women would get together sometimes and crochet or make quilts, and that was your enjoyment in those days. The men would set in the barn, and they would talk and play checkers or throw horseshoes; and the kids, well, they'd run all over the place, chasing and hiding on each other. It didn't cost a lot of money to have fun then, and I think it was more fun to it.

❧

There was more time to have fun in the winter when there wasn't so much work to do.

❧

When somebody got a radio, now that was something great. Everybody would go in the evening and set around and listen to it. All the neighbors would go over and set. It was something to hear all that stuff come out of that box. People would set by the hour and just listen to it.

❧

I remember I was fascinated when I first saw a pair of roller-skates. Of course that was in the city, and I think it was a boardwalk – a sidewalk made with boards – and they skated on there. I wanted a pair of skates so bad, but I had no place to skate. There weren't nothing but dirt and mud where I lived.

❧

Birthday parties were a big thing. You couldn't wait for somebody to have a party and invite you to come.

❧

I'll bet you never heard of Hucky-Bucky-Booster. It was a game we played. You'd take and hide something, and everybody would go and look for it. It was usually something small you would hide, and you played it mostly in the house when you couldn't go out.

■

Doctors & Medicine

"Look here now... you're working on the wrong end."

I was supposed to have my birthday one time on a Sunday, and this man said, "It'll be a hundred years before you'll have another birthday on a Sunday." I never did forget that, but he was just running his head. I had one this year on a Sunday, or last year, one. He was with a medicine show. It was 1918 or '20, around there.

Man, those fellers would put on a show. There'd be a crowd there every night – clowns and all that mess up there. They'd kick up a whole lot of fuss, and then they'd go around and sell these 'erbs. They'd send three or four out in the crowd with bottles of something trying to sell it: liniment, 'erbs, rattlesnake oil, and all that. Ditch water is what it was, I guess.

They'd come through about canning season when the cannery people got their shanties filled up. They knowed when to come, when all this crowd of migrants got in them shanties along about the middle of summer. Them medicine fellas would make a killing.

Pop would say, "Let's go to the show tonight."

I'd say, "Yeah, let's go."

They had 'em in town where there was an open place. They'd have little wagons, and they'd have doors to let down and make a platform, and they'd get up there and sell that stuff. It was a time of it.

I remember this one fella: He had a pair of horses to a wagon, a covered wagon, and a platform out the back. He'd get up there and do a little act, play a little music;

then he'd get out there and peddle what he had. He sold all kinds of liniments and pills and that kind of stuff; had half a dozen or eight kinds of stuff he was selling. After he'd do his little act, he'd go around through the crowd, show them what he had, tell them what it'd do, and try to sell it. Then he'd get back on the stage and sing another song, do a little dance or something, come up with another thing, and go around and try to sell that. If he had eight or ten people, he could sell four or five bottles of the stuff.

Them medicine shows was about the only entertainment you had then, and he was the only doctor you ever got to see. Course he weren't no doctor, not a real one, but sometimes – I have a great mind – you was just as well off with him as the ones you got today.

&

When we got the first doctor in these parts, he would come to the house for a dollar, and he'd give you medicine too. He carried all kinds of pills in a great old black bag.

&

When I first went to a doctor, he had a room where he looked at you, and it had shelves from the floor to the ceiling on every wall except where the door was. And them shelves was filled with medicine. He kept everything anybody could need right there. There weren't hardly no drugstores in them days; didn't need none. They should think about it again.

&

Today everybody got to go to a doctor and spend all this money. If my parents got a cut or something, they put something on it or take something and heal it right up.

I got this book. It's a real book. It tell you what to do for a cut or gas or boils or a heart problem – everything.

That book tell you what to do every time.

ਣ

I used to have them boils real bad. I still got scars all down my legs. They used to call me Lazarus or somebody. I took molasses and sulfur. They mixed it up some way, and I'd take a tablespoon of that, and damn if it didn't cure the boil business. Some rub fat meat on 'em, but I never tried no fat meat.

When I'd have an earache, Pop would get up at night and smoke his old pipe and blow smoke in your ear. Some would pour boiling water over pine shats and blow that steam in your ear, but Pop, he used the old RJR or Duke's Mixture remedy.

One thing we never had no cure for was the flu. It was 1918 and 1919 nearly everybody had the flu. It wiped out whole families. We didn't have no doctors, and no medicine could help a bit; just had quinine and British Oil. Now that was something terrible. It was a black liquid, black as molasses and almost as heavy. People used to take it for sore throats and cold in the lungs and what not. That's the first thing you'd do: get the British Oil. It come in a little old square bottle.

But the influenza cleaned out a lot of people in this territory. Sometimes it would clean out a whole family. God! It cleaned Scott's family out. It didn't miss one. It took the mother and the kids too. It was the first double funeral I ever seen.

ਣ

I just ain't been right since last winter. I seen this doctor, and he give me this medicine. Now I ain't nothing for taking pills. This doctor would have you throw 'em in just like you was stuffing up a rat hole. But I took some, and every time I take it, my head gets to roaring, and I gets dizzy. I fell out one time when I was just setting in

135

the chair; fell right out. I tell this doctor there's something wrong with that medicine, and he says, "Now it's an important one for you to take." Shit! Every time I'm feeling good and take that pill, it's go to work on me. So I take it and take it, and it make me sick every time. So I quit. I seen him the other day and he says, "You taking your medicine?"

I says, "Yeah."

ze

My neck was hurting all the time and had knots on these glands in there. I could take two aspirins and a glass of Coca Cola, and that kills the pain, but I don't want to get in the habit of it. It ain't nothing but dope. You take two aspirins and a Coca Cola, and you're filling up with dope. I was debating that I had to pick a doctor somewhere.

So I heard about this new doctor, and I went over there with my neck hurting. He took all my clothes off and put me in this little white gown and set me down there. So about the first thing he told me: he wants a pap test; he wants a mammogram; he wants a blood test. I said, "Look here now, it's my neck what's hurting. You're working on the wrong end." So I haven't been back to him anymore.

I got some Bufferin, and it's really helping my neck, and I got a scarf around it. The doctor who delivered my children and my grandchildren always told me to never let the wind blow on my neck, and he's give me enough old black Iodex salve to rub on my neck to paint a barn with. It's just as black and smeary as could be. I said I'm not going any farther.

ze

You know, my old pony has got arthritis. A man stop the other day and said it wasn't arthritis; said it was founders. Said when they got that founders, they keep their head down to graze, and it makes her shoulders all sore so she can't walk. Shit! She got arthritis all over. I had a great mind to tie a copper wire around her legs, but she got so much hair it won't do no good. It helps my arthritis, but I ain't got all that hair.

I made a wire bracelet for Billy, but he said it never helped him none. Shit! He never kept it on there. He said it crippled him. You got to keep it on there a month or so at least. He wanted me to make him a flat copper band so it wouldn't dig him. I said, "I ain't gonna make you nothing more. You want another bracelet, you make it yourself."

&

I got a toothache since Sunday, and my head feels big as a barn. Reminds me of the old saying: "Big head, big wit; little head, not a bit."

We had no dentists when I was growing up, no way to get to them, and no money to pay them if we could of. My father went to a man, and he would pull a tooth. He was just a farmer, but he was a jack-leg, a jack-of-all-trades. He had some kind of a pair of nippers, and he'd pull them out. He didn't have nothing to give you for the pain; he'd just pull them out.

He was a judge too. You had any trouble, you went before him and get it straightened out. I don't know if he was authorized or if he just did it on his own. If you got drunk and got in a fight or whatever, you went before him. He'd put a five-dollar fine on you pretty quick. Whatever tales they might tell you about him, there's a lot of truth in it; I'll bet you that.

&

My teeth were rotten and ached all the time when I was young. Last I had was six pulled over to Easton. I guess that was in the thirties. Some old doctor pulled 'em. It was fifty cents or a dollar. I believe it was fifty cents. I went in there, and he yanked 'em out. He didn't give me nothing for it, and they was hurting like the devil. I came back and put a chew of tobacco in. I was spitting that out and blood, and it never did get sore.

An old man over in Preston made teeth. I think it was nine dollars for a plate. I had a gold cap on one that was pulled, and I kept it. The old man said, "You want that gold one in there?"

I said, "Yeah, put it in there." So it was thirteen-fifty with the gold one on it.

I wore holes in that plate after a time and had some other teeth made down to Salisbury, but I couldn't wear the damn things. I got 'em around here somewheres. They got great, long teeth on 'em. So I went back to this old man in Preston, and I told him, "Look, I done wore a hole in this plate. How about you put a blowout patch on it for me." And that's what he done. I wore holes in it two or three times, and I'd go back and have a blowout patch put on it. That's the truth. This is the same plate I got from that old man in the thirties.

■

Ghosts, Witches & Treasure

"This woman died one time and come back."

Lots of the old people tell how they've heard a knock on the door, and they go, and there's nobody there. It's a token. Then somebody comes and tells them about a death or an accident or something bad.

You can find lots of people who used to see lanterns and faces in the window at night, and nobody would be there.

ba

You used to hear about ghost lights all the time. People would see lights all down below in the marshes. There were a mess of 'em around Robbins and Shorters Wharf and around a cemetery down there. It ain't been long I heard about that again. Nobody ever could catch one as I know. They'd run around out there – them lights would – and they'd go out when you tried to go up to 'em. Of course a lot of people were too scared to go out there.

They had a ghost light over to Hebron one time. People seen this light all through there. Cops seen it. It was a road they called Ghost Light Road, and people would sit and watch for that light to come across the field. We went down one night and set and watched. It was lined up all down that road – people looking. It's only one time we went. We didn't see no ghost or no light.

I never seen a ghost. I've read about 'em, but I can't keep nothing to tell you about it. I haven't seen one, but I've seen some funny things and heard some funny noises. I was riding a horse one night from Walnut Landing by the old church that was over there. It was funny: Every time I come by there at night, that church door would be open. You go by in the daytime, and that door would be shut; but at nighttime, I don't ever remember I went by that it wasn't open. And the graveyard was right there at the corner of it. This night my brother went one way, and I went another. My brother was on a mule, and I was on a horse. We said we were gonna see who gets home first. That old mule just had his one gait, but my horse could fly, so I thought I'd ride up there and see what's with that door. It was eleven o'clock at night, and there wasn't a lantern anywhere 'tween Walnut Landing and home, not a spark for miles, nothing but stars. I drove that horse up to that great slab out front of the door. She snorted and blowed and took off at a gallop. I never did find out what was in there.

The worst I was ever scared though: back of our house, back there in the woods, the people who lived there before had dragged every old animal they ever had back there. There were bones everywhere, and there was an old mill in there with a great big sawdust pile. I was coming by that sawdust pile one night, and it was just as ca'm as it could be. I commenced to hearing this sound, something like a cow bellow, way off. And that sound kept coming on and coming on. I said, "God! There's something in here come to life," and I flew home. Come to find out it was an old house way over to Frases, and this man's son had a cornet, and he was blowing it. Some things you can explain, and a lot of things you can't explain.

ૐ

Them ghost lights in the marsh are real; that's not a superstition. Lots of people seen them. Some have died because of them lights. Some watermen has drowned. But if you look for them, if you go out there and set just to see them, you won't see them. You never can go out to find them. They won't come then. It's when you're not thinking about it, that's when they come.

୬

People talk about lights in the marsh – ghost lights. I never took much stock in them. That's certain times in the year, certain places where the moon or the sun was late evenings or nights. It looks like a fire, just like a small fire. It's a reflection from the salt water, that's really what it was – a little light somewhere between sundown and dark. After the sun's almost gone or a bright moonlight night, it's a certain place with the moon shining on it. You could see 'em.

Some people say it's glowing balls, and they move around. Well, that would be because it had a breeze or a wind move the water a little. Ca'm night it didn't move; move if it had a little wind. I've seen 'em several times.

There's some say it's gas of some kind. Well, there is gas in gas marshes, but, you know, the elements have some funny ideas. Funny things happen, you know. You can't always figure 'em out. You do have gasses in the marshes in certain places, some kind of gas. I don't know. I'm not smart enough to know what kind of gas. But anyway, that will have a reflection on the water.

Well, a lot of this stuff was just somebody playing a prank anyway. Nothing unusual about all that.

୬

This woman died one time and come back. They buried her, and she come back. It was a preacher's wife. She had a ring, and there was some value to it, and they left it on when they buried her. Everybody knew that, and somebody dug up her grave that night to get that ring. When they went to get it off, she sat right up. Well, they took off   I would too – and she got up and went on home. Now you know that preacher was surprised. They

141

say she lived two, three more years after that. The next time they put her down, I guess she stayed then.

ᨒ

They buried a boy down below. He was sick, and they thought he died. After they buried him, they would hear a boy cry and scratch on the windows and on the walls. After a time went by, a hurricane come and washed out a lot of graves, and the boy's coffin washed out and come open. You could see in there where he had scratched the coffin to get out. Of course they couldn't hear him.

It was a long time people would hear him at night. I don't know what become of it. Well, I think I do remember they said it stopped when that coffin come open.

ᨒ

There's a graveyard on Kirwins Neck Road. You'd go down to that graveyard at twelve o'clock at night, right on the dot of twelve. You'd have a black hat on and carry a globe lantern. I forget what the old man's name was, but you'd stand over his grave and holler down and say, "Mr. so-and-so, what did you die for?"

He'd say, "Nothin'."

ᨒ

It used to be told there were some big boundary markers, great old monuments to show property lines. Some of those old stones had writing on. They said that every time those boundary stones would hear a rooster crow, they would turn around.

ᨒ

There's ghosts in the marsh. People swear it. A lot of 'em is mixed up with treasure. Old Marcellus Hurley seen a man toting a chest out in the marsh, and he walked past him and never looked one way or the other. It was

142

like he could see right through him, and then he just walked off right across that creek. There's an island they call Ghost Island. Some think the ghost is old man Lewis, him that built the old house below Cokeland.

And the old house down there, they say that's haunted too. It was, I guess. They heard all kinds of noises down there and somebody walking around. Several people say they heard that. Then somebody found gold there, and after that they never did hear nothing again. They say the ghost was watching after that gold, and when they found it, he went away then. Maybe it was old man Lewis.

There's a lot of stories about Big Liz. Some say she was a witch, but I guess she was just an old woman. She was a slave, or she worked for this man, and he was for the South in the Civil War. He had a mess of gold and stuff, and he thought the army was coming for him. He's supposed to buried it all there in Greenbrier Swamp. Liz – she helped him bury it, and then he cut her head off so she couldn't tell nobody. Now that's the truth. That really happened. But they say her ghost is still down there, and she carries her head under her arm. The kids go down there at night, there by DeCoursey Bridge – that's Greenbrier Swamp there – and they blink their car lights. She's supposed to come out then carrying her head. I guess that's the kids just trying to scare somebody. You used to hear a lot about it, but I don't hear much no more.

People would always come around and say there's money buried here and there's money buried there. They were always going out and dig for money. Right in this swamp between here and Indiantown, they say Frank Milligan found money there. I had a good saddle horse when I lived over there, and I'd ride all those roads, and I'd fox hunt over there. They said he dug some money up right close to the road, and there was a hole there. It looked like it was rusty. Old Frank did go to Washington a couple of days after that, and he was one never went anywhere except in his buggy to town. Frank did have some money. Course he worked hard all the time cutting cordwood, and they said they lived on summer herrings; that's all they'd eat. He'd go down to the river and catch 'em.

I think there's some gold buried around this county. There was another treasure supposed to be buried down in Greenbrier, and they put a spike in a tree to mark it. They say they brought it up the bay in a ship and come in the Transquaking River to the swamp, and that's where they buried it. They put an iron spike in a big oak tree to mark the place, but they never come back for it. One day they brought some big oaks out of the swamp to the mill there in Bucktown. They were running one of them logs through that mill, and it struck a iron spike and busted the saw all to pieces. I guess they looked for the stump but never could match it up, as bad as that place is. I don't guess nobody'll ever find it now.

&.

There used to be lots of stories about witches and ghosts, always somebody seeing somebody with no head. You be riding down the road in the buggy in the nighttime – they seen this and they seen that. And if a fellow had a cow and it went dry, they'd say there was a spell on it, and they'd want to burn somebody out they thought was a witch. You don't hear that no more.

&.

They used to say that cramps come from a witch doing black magic on you, sticking pins in a doll or something. When I woke up this morning, I had cramps in both feet; felt like it was pulling the leaders right out from my knees. I got so I could get a hold on one after a while, and I twisted on it, and it finally left. I don't know why some witch would be trying to get after me.

&.

Some used to say the old granny women were witches. They were bad about it. They'd talk about 'em and ridicule 'em. I don't know hardly how to explain it. Somebody would say, "That granny woman, she's a witch. She done this, and she done that, and she done the other." When I got to be a teenager, a lot of that died out; but when I was a boy, it was a little strong on some people, being witchy and putting spells on you and stuff like that. After I took on a little size, I didn't put much stock into it. But some of the older ones – I'd hear them talking – they really believed that somebody would put a spell on 'em.

ঽ৾

They say a broomstick will take care of a witch; it will keep her away. If you wanted to keep a witch out of the house, you would take and cross two brooms in the doorway. Or if you had just one broom, you would put it across the doorway. A witch would never step over a broomstick.

ঽ৾

The only witch I ever knowed of – Pappy would tell us about that – she lived down to Bestpitch Ferry. They say she could fly and walk on the water. She never done that if somebody was watching; only done it when nobody would be around. She didn't want nobody to know she was a witch, I guess. But one fella seen her. He follered her one time and hid in the grass, and he seen her walk across the river there. She just went right across and never made no wake. Pappy said he heard that down to Jesse Walls one time. Them boys down there would talk about all that stuff.

And she had a boy, I guess. He never wore no clothes they told, and he lived wild down there in the marsh. People would see him with their cows. They called him Cow Man. Somebody finally caught him, or they got him and tamed him, and he lived in a little house or a little shanty down there. And he got married, and he lived down there

145

till he was almost a hundred. I guess he was still living in the Forties. They say he was that witch's boy. I don't know who his pappy was. If she was a witch, maybe he never had no pappy.

&

You know, sometimes you wake up in the morning, and it's like you never been to sleep at all. It's like you was working the whole night long. They used to say that was from a witch would be riding you all night. One old man would always say, "My God, I's all wore out. Some witch been a-riding me last night." A witch, you know, she could turn herself into anything she wants, and you too. She could get in the house through a crack. She could turn herself into a bug or a worm and crawl right inside any house, and she could turn you into a horse or a mule and ride you. You heard lots of stories about witches turning people into horses and riding 'em till they'd be ready to fall right out, and they weren't worth nothing the next day. The old people believed all that stuff, but you don't hear much of it no more. They had charms to keep witches off. A chestnut was one thing they carried, and all kinds of dried-up stuff.

&

Whenever your stock got sick or died, or when people got sick, or if you had a fire, or if the crops went bad, they used to say that was some witch made a spell against you. They believed some awful things, and they done some awful things if they thought somebody was a witch or made spells against somebody. People took the law in their own hands. There's houses been burned and people missing.

&

Silver – they said a witch just can't abide no silver. You give a witch a silver needle, and she'd drop it and scream. The only way you could kill a witch – it's what they always

146

said – was with silver bullets.

Witches could walk on water and wouldn't drown. It's a way to find if somebody is a witch: if you throw her in water.

You could find out another way; I forget exactly how it was now. I think you put some nails – I don't know if they had to be silver or something – but you drove them in a bench or a seat of some kind, and you set her on that by the fire. Make up a real hot fire, and if she could sit there and not be hot or be burned, then you'd know she was a witch.

ᔢᵃ

It was an old black man – his name was Fairfax – and they said he would put a spell on you. Everybody was afraid of him, even after he died. He had some bad power. It's what caused that man to lose all his hair that time. His boat broke down by Seven Oaks Point, and he walked up through that woods, and he had to come there by Fairfax's house. Course Fairfax was dead then, but his old house was still there. A man came out Kirwins Neck Road and met him, and he was running right wide open. He couldn't stop him. Right after that his hair started falling out. They took him everywhere. It was some hospital in Baltimore told him the only thing they could figure was he'd been scared real bad. Every bit of his hair fell out, every string of it. He was just as bald as the palm of my hand.

■

More Superstitions

"The luck's in the Lord, and the devil's in the people anyhow."

I had a sister-in-law; there wasn't either superstition that she didn't know. She was a character. She was right off her feet. You heard about not having a woman come in the house on New Year's. Well, every year I'd call her up, and I'd say, "Mabel, I'll be over there New Year's to visit you."

She'd say, "Oh God, no! Don't come that day!" Lots of them believed that. See a woman coming, my God, they'd leave home before they'd let them in.

I've heard one say, "Go back honey! I like you, but don't you come in here now." But some say if a man and a woman go together, and the man goes in first, the bad luck's gone then.

I say if a woman is all that much bad luck, then why do the men want them so bad anyway?

❧

My mother used to say that her grandfather would just as soon see the devil come to his door on New Year's as see a woman come.

❧

You had to have black-eyed peas on New Year's for luck. Mom always had 'em. And you wore something new and shook the change in your pocket; made it rattle. It would bring plenty of money for the rest of the year.

❧

Mom always told us we was supposed to take Christmas decorations down by such and such a day in January or you had bad luck all year. I think there's plenty would be in trouble these days. This one fella just turns 'em off. Next year he turns 'em on again. They stay up all year, and he ain't had no more bad luck than me as I can see.

&

I heard where some would know the weather when they look at the goosebone, but we just had the wishbone. You know that: One would take ahold on each side and pull it apart. The one with the long end would get the wish. They call that the shovel, and they say the one with the shovel will live the longest. He has something to bury the other with.

&

You go to see Miss Edith, you better not hang your hat on her doorknob. That's the worst kind of bad luck to her. Yes sir, she'll tell you something if you do that.

&

We was up to Mabel's one time, and somebody laid their hat on the bed. That was one thing she didn't know. Somebody said, "Mabel, did you know it was bad luck to lay a hat on the bed?"

"Oh God, no!" she said. "I didn't know that." But I'll tell you one thing: that hat come off the bed, and it wasn't long about it either.

&

You gotta be careful about brooms. A lot of people is afraid about brooms. If you start sweeping the floor and my cousin's around, he'd get out of the way fast; he'd get right up and leave. Said he'd go to jail for sure if you hit him with the broom. Course he used to sell a lot of whiskey then, so maybe he had a reason to be afraid about that.

I've heard if you got something on your plate and you reach out to get some more – forget all about you got some there – people say, "Uh huh, you're gonna have company." A lot of people say that.

My grandmother always said that night air was bad for you. She said her mother told her it was poison. I don't believe that, but it will stop you up and give you a cold if it's too damp and chilly.

When I was a kid, we always looked for four-leaf clovers. It was good luck. And the five-leaf clover was supposed to be bad luck. I found them now and then too. Sometimes I had good luck, and sometimes I had bad, and ain't that the way it always is, clovers or no clovers?

I was taking Mom and Pop to Felton one time. After we got up there aways, Mom remembered something she left on the zink by the pitcher-head pump. We come back, and I went in and got it. When I come back out, there was Pop setting down by the door with his legs crossed. I said, "Pop, what are you doing setting there?"

He said, "Anytime you have to turn around and go back somewhere, well now, you had better sit right down and cross your legs to cross off the bad luck."

The old ones all knew that whenever you start for someplace and must go back, you have to sit down and cross your legs and get the bad luck out of the way. When you stop and go back, that breaks the circle. Anytime you

150

break the circle, that's bad luck, and you should sit right down and say a charm. You can say, "Here I sit, now bad luck quit." You count to ten and it's O.K.

ða

If two people were walking and come to a post, and one walk on one side and one on the other side, you cut your love in two. Oh yeah!

ða

Crowing chickens was mostly bad luck. If you would bring the chicken inside in the kitchen, you could find out if it was bad luck or if it was O.K. You go to one corner and set the chicken so its tail is in the corner. Then you turn that chicken over and over from that corner to the other corner like you would do a somersault. If the tail was in the corner when you got across, that was O.K.; you could keep her. But if the head come up in that corner, then you chopped it off. That one was nothing but bad luck.

ða

If you run into somebody was cross-eyed years ago, they'd say you'll come up on the short end. You had to spit through your fingers to get rid of the bad luck. You never hardly see nobody with crossed eyes no more. When I was a kid, there was a mess of people cross-eyed. I guess they get them straightened now if they're born that way.

ða

They always said not to cut your fingernails on a Friday, and you shouldn't cut 'em on a Sunday either. Monday was best, but it was dangerous anytime. If somebody got the parings, they could put a bad luck charm on you.

ða

If a black cat crosses you on the right going to the right,

you best turn around, because it's nothing but bad luck. If it's going to the left, it ain't quite as bad. I seen Babe turn around more than twice, a black cat was crossing him.

❧

A black cat is bad luck anytime, but there's ways you can get rid of his spell. I had a cousin would go back home and cross her legs six times and then start out again, and that would cast off the bad luck. You can spit in a hat too. "Spit in a hat kills the black cat," something like that you say. One man carried a hat for just that reason. He kept it in his car everywhere he went.

❧

I've heard Pop say it many a time: He'd start down the road with his horse cart or derby the first day of the week and meet a colored woman – he'd rather run up on the devil hisself as meet a colored woman on the road first thing on a Monday morning. That brought bad luck all the rest of the week .

❧

If it rains on Easter Sunday, it'll rain for seven Sundays. I always heard that. If it rains on Whitsunday – when is Whitsunday anyway? If it rains on Whitsunday – I forget now how that one goes. I don't know what Whitsunday is. I believe if it rains on Whitsunday, it'll rain for forty days and forty nights. My God, that's the flood, ain't it? When is Whitsunday? It's around huckleberry time, I believe – Whitsunday, ain't it? It should be in the Farmers' Almanac. I got one; I'll check it.

❧

My uncle always used to eat fish from the head to the tail. It was for some kind of luck. He said fish was brain food. I can eat 'em, but I'd rather not. I guess that's why I don't have any sense. He would always say to throw the first fish back and not to count how many you catch. That way you would make a big catch. I don't follow that unless it's a little perch or a toadfish.

≈

You sing before breakfast, you'll cry before bed.

≈

I give some sticks of sassprus wood in a pile to Lewis' wife one time. She said, "Oh my, I don't care to burn that." Come to find out it's a lot of people won't take and burn no sassprus wood. It's just bad luck. I don't know what that is.

≈

Some people would carry a pepper to keep the devil off. Most everybody had something they carried. When we was just little tykers, Mom would put something around our neck. I don't remember now if it was a pepper or a walnut, but she tied something that hung down there. I guess it worked. I never run up on the devil as I know.

It might have been a chestnut. We used to have chestnuts when we were going to school, used to stop and chunk 'em down. There was a great old chestnut tree around the edge of the cripples, but it got some kind of disease, and I guess there ain't a chestnut left in the whole country now.

≈

All the old folks used to carry something or other in their pocket for good luck. A lot of 'em had something was turned just as hard as a stone. Seems to me it was a 'tater that turned to a stone. Sometimes they had it on a string or just in their pocket. I guess you could take an ax and beat it up, but damn if it didn't feel just as hard as a stone to me. I can't figure now anymore just what it was.

≈

I bought a workboat down to Elliott one time. A man was building it for hisself, and I asked him what he'd take for her. He told me, and I said to finish it up and to paint her white with blue trim.

He said, "Man! Now don't go and do that. You don't want no blue on your boat. It's as bad luck as you can get. It's the color of the water," he said, "and you'll have her right under there."

He was real serious too, so we painted the whole thing white.

ै

They always said to not let the moon shine on a child in bed. This woman – poor thing – I think she'll be a hundred her next birthday. She said she had a child die. She said it was stormy that night, and there was no moon shining; but moonlight come right through that window on the child's face in the crib, and it died before morning.

ै

Well, whatever you believe, the luck's in the Lord, and the devil's in the people anyhow.

■

Birds, Beasts, & Bugs

*"I'd rather have the flies and mosquitoes
than the people"*

I could tell you some tales if you had half a day to wait. Uncle Jink Hurley lived down on Guinea. He had a turkey buzzard roosted on the foot of his bed for years. He'd go out in the morning – that old buzzard would – and fly around all day. In the evening he'd come back. He'd come in and roost on the foot of the bed and stay there till next morning. Uncle Jink got that buzzard when it was young, and it roosted there on the foot of his bed for years.

૨ટ

I found a old buzzard nest one time. It was in a holler tree, and there be three or four eggs in there. We kept going back and looking at them till they hatched. They was near about white then, them little buzzards. It look like vomit in there. I said, "Damn! Let's get away from here." I didn't fool around with them no more after that.

૨ટ

There was a lot more buzzards and crows and eagles years ago, forty-to-one over today. Yes sir, a good forty-to-one. When I was a youngster, they used to roost right there in the edge of the branch. I've seen two hundred in there in an evening, trees just full, every stick of 'em.

And crows: when I was a boy, every sunup there'd be a million crows. I'll say a million. I've seen clouds of 'em as far as you could see. They went down there in the evening to roost and come out in the morning.

155

I killed an eagle one morning a long time ago. I don't know why I done it; just done it for meanness sake. I was on Savanna Lake, and the biggest eagle I ever saw in my life come right by me. He come right there. I shot, and he just turned right up. I had an eight-foot oar in that boat, and I laid the eagle on the grass and put that oar across his wings. Just the tips of that oar stuck out either side. I took him and shoved him back in a muskrat lead, shoved him back in there as far as I could get him and went on. I just had to see how big he was.

ぉ

I shot many an eagle, killed many an eagle when I was a boy. There were many of 'em around. One evening I seen one chase a duck. He was right behind that duck, and the duck was quacking and going down and coming up. That eagle kept going on straight after him. He gained a little bit closer and closer all the time. By and by he reached out and got that duck right in the air and kept on going. He had a wing in each claw. That duck was having a fit, but it wasn't no use; the old boy was laying right on him.

I went on down there one morning, and a duck come by. It was early, just getting good and light, and a duck come across there flopping and beating and hollering. I up the gun, and down she fell. And right behind her, ten feet behind her, this eagle come right on her tail; and down he went too. I got 'em both.

ぉ

I had a steel trap one time with good link chain on it. I had it setting on fast land on hard bottom, and that pole was down there hard. I was going to my traps. I was close to this one, and an eagle come there. I thought to myself: now there's a rat in that trap, and he's gonna get it. He went down and got that muskrat and come up with him, and he pulled the chain right in two and went on with it. I went there and pulled up that pole, and it had a piece of chain to it about ten inches long. The rat and the trap was gone. Now you know it's a job to pull a muskrat chain in two. He pulled that chain in two and carried the trap and muskrat away. That's how strong he is.

ॐ

When I was a boy, I used to amuse myself with eagles. I watched 'em many a day. It's remarkable what he can do and the way he does it. A man never seen 'em or been around 'em like I was for years and years. They had a nest around the point below me and raised their young ones there. There was always two or three eagles around. I've seen an eagle catch a black duck right in the air.

My grandfather used to be bad about having pets. He had a wild goose, a raccoon, and a bald eagle. He had a nice eagle – a big one – and it used to set on the doorstep. One day he walked up, and that eagle must of been mad. He jumped up and give my grandfather his claws, tore his pants and meat and all. He just clawed right into him. My grandfather said, "I'll fix you." He picked him up and carried him out to the chopping block, chopped his head off, and threw him over the fence.

One morning we carried the cows and horses down to the point and put 'em on the marsh to graze, and there was an eagle's nest on the point. There was a big pine – a forked pine – and the eagles had young ones into it. My father was great about climbing trees. He said, "I'm gonna climb up there and look at them baby eagles." So he started up. He got about halfway up there, and the old eagle come home and started circling around and hollering. The closer he got to that nest, the closer she go to him. It wasn't long before she took her wing and whipped him across the back. Every time she come around, she'd whip him. She made it so hot for him he couldn't get up there. He got about ten feet below that nest and had to quit and come back down. She was whipping on him, I'll tell you that. She was tearing him up.

He was a great coon hunter, my father was. He'd climb the biggest tree you ever seen – a rope around it, and go right up there. I'm telling you: them times was something.

૨૭

I used to watch eagles all the time. I saw two of 'em fight one time, two roosters, and they fit for three or four days. They fit continuously all day long. It was about mating time .

One morning I was going down the ditch bank, and one was standing there right close to the marsh. He was just as bloody as could be, and he couldn't fly. I walked up to him, and he scooted off a little so I couldn't pick him up. Blood was all over his head and down his feathers, and he was so give out he couldn't hardly get out of the way. He was a pitiful looking sight standing there on that ditch bank. I went on. I don't know what happened to him.

૨૭

Them eagles like to eat fish. I watched one eat a carp last fall, his beak just hanging full of them big scales. He kept pulling at it till it was all eaten.

You used to hear a lot of stories about how they steal fish from the osprey. One morning when I was a kid – it was just after sunup, and I was fishing – there come this great old eagle, his wings set up, and his claws pushed out, and him falling like a stone. This osprey had just rose up from behind some grass with a pike in his claws. He seen the eagle and dropped that pike, and he got out of there fast. The eagle snatched up that pike and took off with him. I never will forget that.

It was more than thirty years later that I seen almost

the opposite. This young eagle was eating something out on the mud flat, and he took off with it. Whatever it was, it was dangling some innards about a foot long. He flew off, and here come this osprey behind that eagle and under him. He went straight for that eagle's belly, but he never touched him. The eagle dropped what it had, but the osprey flew off and didn't go after it. The eagle went back down and got it again.

ॐ

When I was a boy, there wasn't no geese. I was sixteen or eighteen years old before I ever saw a wild goose. In my lifetime since then, I've seen wild geese so thick you could kill all you wanted – plenty of 'em. I've seen thousands of 'em on this river; a boat couldn't get through 'em hardly.

Some years after the geese started to coming in, there started some swans coming. Most of the swans would park in Savanna Lake. I've seen 'em in there – thousands of 'em in there. I've seen whole streaks of 'em, all the way as far as you could see almost. But there ain't much in this territory now. Nature's a funny thing. You can't figure what's gonna happen.

ॐ

A man said yesterday he thinks the foxes are coming back. They ain't been nowhere as I know. There's always been plenty. My father used to raise foxes. It used to make me so mad: I'd have to dig foxes, have to dig up the young ones. He raised foxhounds and trained 'em and sold 'em. That was most of his living. When he'd find a den with the old one carrying food in and out, then he knowed they was big enough to feed.

We went down one Sunday morning to dig a den in a pine wood. We dug and dug and hit a root. There was a bull turkle had got underneath that root. He dug in there, and that root pinned him down. He couldn't get out. We cut the root in two, put that turkle in a burlap bag, and brought him home and eat him. He was just thick through his back. Pop bellied him up by the tail and counted him, and he said that turkle was seven years old and was under that root for five years. Now how could a bull turkle last there with a root across his back for five years, and him as fat as butter? I don't tell that story much no more, 'cause everybody says it's a lie. But it's the truth. We never did get any fox out of there.

But that's what my father's business was. He had a pen almost as big as the yard, just full of foxhounds, and he had a house half as big as that just full of young foxes. He'd have eight or ten or twelve foxes in there, and he'd keep 'em there till the fall of the year. If anybody wanted a dog and wanted to try out that dog, he'd turn a fox out. That way he didn't have to go half a day finding one in the woods. He'd set the dog out there and let him run the fox.

But he never wanted the dog to catch the fox. He used to have a little, black mare; run flat out she could. If the dogs got too close to a fox coming across the field, he'd go and fetch that mare. He'd take her out and come alongside that fox, reach down and take that fox by the back of the neck, pick him up, and bring him alongside. That little mare had done it so many times she'd go right alongside, get her head down there, right flat with that fox. He didn't want the dog to catch the fox. He would put him in a sack and take him home and use him again the next day. He was something.

But I will say there were more foxes then. There was more game of everything. My lord! I could go squirreling; wouldn't be gone an hour, and I'd have seven or eight. Now you can't hardly find one to save your life. There ain't no game no more of no kind down in the necks.

&

All the old folks hunted foxes, but they didn't kill 'em;

least ways they didn't want to. If the dogs caught one, they didn't aim for 'em to. It was a big sport. You'd ride horses and buggies and carriages and road carts – them old two-wheeled carts. You'd ride to where you could listen to the dogs.

We took a fella out one time to hear 'em run. Old Paul said, "Just listen to that music. Ain't that beautiful?"

Man listens for a minute or two and says, "I can't hear no music for all them dogs barking."

॰

It used to be illegal to kill a fox if they was in front of the dogs. Old Will lived down below town, and they were running a fox on his place one day. The dogs got too close, and that fox went in the man's stable, and he killed it. They had a time over that.

॰

We dug for foxes one time in a sawdust pile around an old mill. They like to dig their dens in them old sawdust piles. It won't freeze in there, and it's a good place to raise up their young. We dug for half a day in that sawdust and never did find a fox, but we come up on an old skunk. I don't know if it was the end of the hole or not, but it was the end for us.

There used to be a lot more skunks. My God! The place was full of 'em. You used to go coon hunting and the dogs would get after 'em. Phew! You couldn't stay around there. I remember we went back in Peters Swamp one time, and the dogs got on a coon. We thought it was a coon anyway, and it went in a hole in the ditchbank. The dogs got close in there, and that skunk let go and got scent all over 'em. It was a week before you could get near 'em, and the women didn't want us back in the house that night neither.

One run under my pump house one time, and I got to thinking about it. I thought I'm liable to step on that thing

161

going out there in the morning. I'd go down to the barn to milk, you know, before it got light. I thought maybe I could kill him and not kick up too much of a scent, so I got the 410 on down. He was all curled up in there, but I thought I could see his nose. We'd just threshed wheat – hadn't been long – and I had a rick of straw setting in the field by the barn. Anyhow, I shot. Good God! It stunk so bad I had to come out of there fast. After the scent cooled down a little bit, I got a pitchfork and carried him out there behind the straw rick. I said, "I'll bury you tomorrow." Good God! It was hot that night, and everybody had their window open; and the wind was blowing out of the south. Everybody for a mile had to close all their windows.

ta

People say that muskrats will eat a marsh right up, but I don't believe it. They would gotta be terribly thick to do it. The marsh has a way of growing back every year.

I've seen the muskrats feed many a time. He picks the root up in his front feet and looks at it. Then he sees if anybody's looking at him. Then he takes the bark off, takes his teeth and pulls that off and spits it out. When he gets down to the heart – that's white – he'll eat that. He'll take a mouthful or two and looks around again. He's always look- ing to see if anybody looks at him, and every time he takes two or three bites, he takes it down and washes it with his feet. I've seen him do that many a time; set in my boat and watched him feed on roots. It amused me.

I'll tell you one thing: He's a clean animal. He's every bit particular about his food. It's clean as a whistle, but he'll wash it again. You needn't ever be afraid to eat him. Muskrat's good eating. It's sweet meat, a whole lot better than rabbit. I was pretty near raised on it.

ta

This man – Captain Lewis was his name – had a big

gray squirrel. It was a male squirrel, one of them cat squirrels. He'd sit in his big chair and fool with that thing. He'd always have something in his pocket: two or three grains of corn or a peanut. That old squirrel would get up on his shoulder and go through his pockets and get what he had in there.

One day Captain sat back in his chair, and that old squirrel jumped on his shoulder and went through his pockets, and he didn't have nothing in there for him. The old squirrel got mad and bit him right through the ear, and he jumped down and run up to the top of a tree. Captain got his old musket down, and he said, "Damn you!" Shot him right out of that tree.

⸙

When we lived on that farm over in Indiantown, my brother and I caught some squirrels. We was always doing something. Next to the other farm there were several trees down a turning row, and we went out there with the mules and a cart one day to get a shock of fodder. We backed in there and got it loaded, and then we seen this squirrel run in that turning row – a great big old squirrel. I guess he was in one of them shocks of fodder. We took to chasing him, and he climbed this tree. We'd finally get him to jump out, and he'd go to another tree. We fooled with that thing till we give him out. Damn if we wasn't give out too. We caught him then and carried him up.

We fixed up a coop with wire and put him in there, and we put that on the porch. After a while we got him a little bit tame, but it was an old squirrel, and you ain't taming him much. Sometimes we let him out on that screened porch. We had shutters on a window – a great, tall window. We'd turn him out in there, and he'd go up that shutter, "zip," and set on top of it.

Later on we caught a young one when they were hatched out. We caught him back in the woods and brought him up.

163

We give the old one to somebody 'cause he wanted to bite you all the time. That little one got right smart tame and would come and eat out of your hand. We had him on the porch too, but if you'd leave the door open he'd go upstairs and everywhere. But most of the time he's just run up that shutter, "zip," and set there.

ð

This is the truth, so help me Lord, but I don't often tell it 'cause nobody in the world will believe it: When I was a youngster – I guess I must have been seventeen – an old man run a mill down in the neck, down next to the marsh. He was cutting pine timber in there, and I was working for him. I was a handyman. Anything he wanted done, I'd do it. We had two pairs of mules there and two carts for to haul logs up. Well, there come up a swarm of sheep flies, and they were so bad that nobody in this world wouldn't believe it. I took a pair of mules out that stable one morning to work, and I carried 'em to give 'em water. The flies was so thick they broke loose and run back to the stable. The flies on 'em were just as thick like a blanket. You couldn't put your finger on them mules but you put it on a fly. They were thick as bees around a hive, swarms of 'em. I never got them mules out of that stable for fifteen days. There wasn't no way you could get 'em out. You try to get 'em out, and they rear up, blating and hollering, and run back. We had to carry water to 'em with a pail for two weeks.

ð

Whenever the flies would get bad, a real down-necker would dress the old mules up in burlap and tow bags and smear some pine tar on there. Sometimes you put it right on his hide.

ð

In the old times in the fly season, people would first put on their boots. Then they'd put their overalls outside of them, put on a big heavy jacket, gloves and all, and get some sweetgum branches. They'd cut off forked branches and put them over top of their heads and let them hang down. They'd just have a little place between the leaves to see where they was going, and you could see them coming through the woods with their heads so big around. The flies would be so think – just millions of them – and they'd walk along with no problem at all. I seen it over and over again down in the necks.

ᾳ

People who lived down below used to say it: If they wanted to go to town come a Saturday night, they'd look down the lane first. If they couldn't see down there, then they'd take the old shotgun and shoot down there a couple of times to clear the mosquitoes out. Then they'd come on up.

ᾳ

I'll tell you one thing: the mosquitoes were bad when I used to go down to the Island. I'd be talking to an old man born and raised down there, and I'd be beating with a brush all around the back of my head and face. He'd tell me, "Son, all you do is make 'em mad, beating on 'em like that." After a while his face would get covered with mosquitoes. He'd take a hand and just wipe 'em off, slow like.

ᾳ

I used to carry coal oil to this fella's place. Damn! You'd think you were going through the woods. He never even cut a road through it. I'd sit up in the cab and shut both my eyes – bushes all over – but I'd get up there. That was the greatest place I ever seen.

He caught mosquitoes and sold 'em. He'd put so many in a jar and sell 'em to somebody. I guess they wanted to

165

know how long they lived or something. I guess they was making some kind of chemical, and they put it in there to see if it would kill 'em. I don't know what, but I know one thing: he had jars setting all around. They say there's still jars just full of dried skeeters up that attic, and him dead all these years.

❧

I had a girlfriend on the Island when I was seventeen or eighteen, and I'd go down there evenings. People went in the house about half an hour before sundown, closed up everything tight – no light or nothing – and sat there in the dark. When you went outside, the mosquitoes swarmed all over you. You couldn't keep 'em out of your mouth and eyes. You'd get your nose and mouth full when you breathed. But those people lived there till they were seventy and eighty. They were born into it, and they learned how to handle it.

❧

Walking through that tall grass down in the marsh, I seen mosquitoes come up just like a fog, just like smoke. You couldn't see the sun for mosquitoes. I'd have an old straw hat on, gloves, net tied all on my head, and I'd wade through there. You wouldn't believe how many mosquitoes would come up unless you seen them. They'd come up just like the grass was on fire. People today don't know what mosquitoes are.

❧

When the pasture would get bad and the cows would go dry, I'd carry them in the marsh. I had a place in there on an island for them to graze. Sometimes the flies and mosquitoes would get so bad the cows would get down in the creek and drown theirselves. Those cattle would get in the creek till there was nothing but their nose sticking

166

out. They'd stay there till they got so weak they couldn't get out. They'd drown right there. I went down one time; had eight or ten cows there, and every one was in the creek. Three of them was drowned dead. I got the rope around the rest and pulled them out with a mule.

❧

I'm not much for the city, not me. I'd rather be to the marsh or the woods someplace. I'd rather have the flies and mosquitoes than the people.

■

Snakes

"I'll tell you one thing: that old man had a nose."

Lord, I hate snakes! There was a snake in my 'maters not long ago. I tore up many a hill with the pitchfork trying to kill it. He had black rings around his tail. I never did see but that much of him, and I never seen one before with stripes around his tail. They was as wide as my little finger and black. I just tore up them hills a-beating and a-hammering in there after him. Shit! It don't make no difference; I don't have no 'maters noway. I don't know what kind it was; don't know the names of 'em nohow. I know we have the blacksnake and the copperhead and the cornfield snake – that old spotted snake – and the field viper has got stripes or spots or something. They're a yellowish cast and got black on 'em, and they ain't too long. I don't remember now. I ain't seen one for a while and ain't looking for none. Then there's the water snake; I just call 'em water snakes. I'll tell you: I'm scared of snakes. Cold chills run all over me when I see 'em.

I heard Pop say way back in the olden times when we had corn in the corn crib: "Now don't kill the blacksnake." It would catch the mice in his corn, you know.

When he told me that, I said, "Well, you do the feeding then. Damn if I'm going in there with them snakes."

He always said, "They won't hurt you."

I said, "Well, maybe no, but they'll make me hurt myself."

❧

168

My brother wasn't afraid of snakes. He used to be out there plowing and plow one out. He would catch it and tie a string around its tail and fasten it to something in the barnyard. The old snake would run all around out there.

ね

Lord-a-mighty! It's been a bad day so far. Man a'ks me clean that ol' house over to Hawkeye. I goes in there, and there lay this great ol' snake frame on the floor. No way I gonna stay there with that ol' snake frame. They come back for that frame, you know. I ain't the one gonna be in there when he come back for it. No sir! Don't need no job that bad. No sir! Don't need that job noway.

ね

A fella come down here last deer season, him and his wife. He's got a big old panel truck. Course he had all his food stacked in there and everything else he wanted to bring. He stopped in here on his way to his trailer. Didn't seem a minute, he was back over here again. He took all his stuff in and set it down, and his wife looks in there and says, "Damn, there's a snake in here. Here's a shed."

"Goddamn!" he said, "Let's get this stuff out of here."

He loaded it all back in the truck and come over here. He wanted to know if I had a hose would go over the end of his exhaust pipe. He was gonna kill that snake. She found that shed – it was a little one anyway – and right away they have to get out of there. The snakes gets in all those trailers in the summertime, but he gets out by now, I guess.

ね

Snakes will get in your house. The tiniest crack – that snake will be in there. Ma had one in her clothesbasket one time. Old clothesbasket set in the closet, you know. She went on in there to pick that basket up – I heard her

169

scream and holler. A big old blacksnake rolled out that thing. God! Scared her near to death.

꩜

Snakes get in Mildred's house over there, and it's no wonder. Open as it is, anything can get in there. She say she can smell 'em. She say, "They're in here somewhere; I can smell 'em." She gets all nervous about it. God! I'd chink every hole; I'd get that nervous. I'll tell you: Both of us wouldn't stay in that same house if I knowed about it. No sir!

꩜

Jimmy had a snake in the walls last week. Carter run through the field with his chopper and run one out – a big old blacksnake – and it run right under the house. He said he knew what would happen; it's always the same thing. About an hour after that he heard it slide across the ceiling. They get under there and go right up through a crack in the walls. He said he had one lived in there all winter; he believed it did.

Next day – he said he guessed he shouldn't tell me or I won't go down no more – he stepped out the front door. He said he don't know why he looked up just then, but there was this old blacksnake with his head just sticking out under the eaves up there. I would of shot the roof off, I guess, if it been my house. I said, "You think I would sleep in there with that?" He said he don't sleep in the attic nohow. Not me! It don't take but a tiny hole, and he finds his way down to where I was.

꩜

It's the teeniest hole – that snake will get in. I got my wheat drill out one day, and I had a quart can in it. I kept looking in that can. I said, "Now what do you suppose that is?" and I kept looking and looking. That can had a hole just about as big as my finger where I poured the oil out, and I kept looking and kept looking. I said, "You know one thing: that's a snake in there." I went to home and got my automatic, and I brought it down and shot him. He rolled right out of there. He was a great, long one, and how he got rolled up in that quart can I don't know.

ã

There was a lot of snakes when I was a boy, plenty of snakes. I guess there still is. My father put the ox to the cart one time and sent me in the woods to get a load of logs, and I went on down there. Snakes in them logs – I killed eleven snakes under one load of logs. They was big as my thumb and two foot long. Had a head sticking out everywhere, and I took the ax and went to chopping heads off and chopping 'em up. I killed eleven, put the chain around the logs, picked 'em up, and come up with 'em. I don't know how many more was under there.

ã

We were falling corn once. Used to cut corn down by hand in them days and put it in piles the whole length of the field. Then we'd put it in shocks. First thing you done: you pulled the blades off and wrap 'em up for feed. Then you cut the tops off and done them up in bundles. Then you cut the cob off and laid that down in piles. One day we were cutting corn. I picked up a turn and had something was cool in my hand. I thought I just had another stalk of corn under there, but it started kind of wiggling. I looked down, and I had hold of a snake. I had hold of him, and his head was hanging down. Well, I pretty soon put that down. But he weren't poison. He was just an old, black-footed cornfield snake.

ã

Two blacksnakes – I'll never forget it. I was plowing

171

with a riding plow and three mules. It was in the spring of the year – still cool – and I plowed up these snakes. I said, "What the devil is that?" I stopped and got off. It was two blacksnakes, and they was rolling around and around one another. I was near about to the end of the lane, and there was this sassprus bush growed up there. So I broke that off – it wasn't big enough to kill 'em noway – and raked 'em through the front of the colter. It was a colter on just that one plow. When I started again, the plow raised right up over 'em. That old colter wouldn't even nick 'em. It wouldn't cut 'em none. They's tough. They won't die till the sun goes down. You can kill 'em and hang 'em on the fence, but they won't die till the sun goes down. It's the God's truth. I seen it many a time.

≈

I come on a baby snake one time, and it struck right out at me. I had gloves on, so I picked him up. He weren't longer than a pencil. That little thing struck right out for my face. He didn't get me, but he struck out just like a big one will. I give him my glove, and he struck it again and again. Finally, he just hung on it and chewed his mouth back and forth. They're born bad is all, nasty from the day they're hatched out.

≈

Last time I went squirreling – it was back over the branch where I have that old toilet for a deer stand. It was cool that morning, and the skeeters wasn't bothering me too much. Well, I seen this thing up there on a limb right by the old toilet. There was this old wild cherry, and the grapevines would grow up there every which-a-way. I said, "Now that looks like a snake on that grapevine," but I couldn't make out whether it was or not. I said, "One thing: I'm gonna shoot you. If you fall out I know you're a snake."

172

"Pow!" Out he comes.

ଈ

You know, a snake can charm a bird. Some say they can charm it right to death. I ain't never see one do it, but I heard a lot of people say they'll really go and do that.

ଈ

Pappy used to say a blacksnake can whip a copperhead. Said he seen a blacksnake and a copperhead go to fighting one time. Said the blacksnake eats some kind of 'erb so the poison don't take hold of him. I don't know what kind of 'erb it was, but Pap knowed what it was.

ଈ

If there was copperheads around here before 1925, I never seen 'em. Some say they got blowed in here from Hurricane Hazel, but they was around before that.

ଈ

I worked around the marsh and the woods and the fields all my life till I was growed. I seen all kinds of snakes, but copperheads was something I never seen until about 1930. First one I seen was in Kraft Neck. I come up the side of the ditch there, and I looked at him. His head was shining just like a Lincoln penny. I said, "That must be a copperhead." So I cut a stick and whacked him and overhauled him. I must of been thirty or thirty-five years old at that time.

Most of 'em are in the pine woods. They do their hunting at night, and they do it in the high woods. A lot of snakes want to get down in the water and mud and look around for frogs and stuff like that, but the copperhead likes it dry.

ଈ

A lot of people say they see copperheads when they're nothing but field vipers, just them little old field vipers.

ॐ

They're poison, them flatheads is, just rank poison. They'll stay right there and rear up and get you. Yeah!

ॐ

We had a great big stump in our yard one time; been there for years, and it decayed so bad. Wasn't any bull-dozers around then to shove it out, so we let it set there. We kept finding these old copperheads, and we was wondering where they was coming from.

I had a man under the house one day fixing my pipe. I looked in there and saw this copperhead crawl across that man's feet, crawl right over his legs. I'm not lying to you. It crawled right over his legs and went on in there. It's the God's truth if I die right here. I was afraid to say anything, you know, afraid he liable to knock his brains out getting out of there. So I let it go. I never did tell him.

But we kept killing 'em from out that stump until we finally shoved it out. That's right where they was raising at. When we shoved that stump out, here come several of 'em right then.

ॐ

I had a snake under the combine head the other year. That was a bad thing. And didn't that snake holler and squeal just like a old raccoon. That was the biggest one we ever got. We were getting ready to put the header on the combine, and that darn thing – they'll squeal, you know. If he's close to you, he'll squeal most of the time. He was in that header, and we didn't know where he was at. Jimmy and Everett was there. Jimmy was right in that header, and man, he come out of there.

He said, "I'll tell you one thing: there's a copperhead

174

in there."

I said, "I thought so. I heard it too."

Jimmy went home and got his shotgun while Everett run a stick up in that header. That snake got to the edge of that header and had his head out. Jimmy cut it right off, and we pulled him out. Oh my God! It was big around as a gallon jug.

≥∞

I had this old combine one time, and there was a sprocket wore out in the throat of her. It was in the summertime, hot as the devil. I said, "Well, I'll take that combine out. I'll take the head off and see if I can put that new sprocket in there." Then I got to thinking about it. I thought there's liable to be a snake in this thing. Several time I backed her out and had a snake in there. I thought I ain't gonna set my rear on the edge of this thing with a snake in there looking right at me. So I looked in, and there he was, a big, black one. Man, he was curled up in a pile. I thought I can't shoot him or I'll blow a hole in the combine. Maybe if I lift that lid and pour some gasoline on him, maybe he'll come out. I had the shotgun out there.

About that time old Freddy come along with the Mills boy. They'd been to a sale. I said, "Come over here; you're the man I want to see. I got a snake in here." I said, "Get a pitchfork or a shovel or something." They went at it. Freddy took the fork and bring him out. The Mills boy had the shovel and beat him up and killed him.

But he had a lump way back in his body. It was seven inches 'cause I measured it. Charles' old cat had been down here and had kittens, and she kept missing 'em. We thought the cat was carrying 'em back up to the house. After a while I got the ax and chopped close to that lump and mashed it out. The last one of them kittens! Hadn't swallowed it too long 'cause the hair wasn't even rubbed off.

≥∞

175

You know how snakes eat? They take and swallow stuff, and then they wrap around a tree or a post and crush it. That's what they do with 'em.

~

An old colored man used to help me. He helped me sort tomatoes and cultivate and stuff. He was living by hisself, and he told me one morning, "Yep," he said, "I slept in that bed all winter." Said, "I felt that knot down there in the end of that bed; felt that knot with my feet every night, but I didn't pay no attention to it." Said, "Come to find out it was a big old blacksnake laying back in there."

All winter long that snake laid in them covers there with him. It's the truth. He told me. It made cold chills run down my back.

~

Pix was down to the cottage two or three years ago, and we was out there crabbing. We was a third of the way across the river, and I says, "There's a snake swimming from the shore there."

"Run over there," Pix says, "and I'll get it." He says, "Give me a paddle and I'll hit it."

And he did hit it, but I says, "That snake ain't dead none."

"Come around," he says. "Go back and I'll get it." He got it by the tail that time and says, "I'll show you how to snap his head off."

I says, "Don't you put it in the boat, and I don't care what you do with it."

Well, he hauled off and give him a crack, cracked him like a whip. It didn't do it. Well, the next time his head flew; I don't know how far. Yes sir! A big old blacksnake.

~

There's some snakes over in this swamp older than I

am. It's a world of snakes in there. Buck bulldozed up a great old one when he cut the roads through there.

Old Dorsey said he was back there huckleberrying one time – he was a great huckleberrier anyway. Back there one day, he says he got tired and thought this was a big log, and he set down on it, set right on it. He said it started to moving. He said he had his shotgun but was afraid to shoot it. He said its eyes was as big as saucers. Scared of snakes as he was, he sets down on one. Course he was lying. He'd climb a tree to tell a lie before he'd tell the truth standing on the ground.

❧

This old fellow Monroe – course he's dead now – he lived back there aways on that dirt road. Him and Clyde was doing something one day, setting out 'maters or something. Anyway, they were walking out there, and Monroe said, "I smell a copperhead, Mr. C."

And Clyde said, "Aw," but he looked. Sure enough, there it lay, and they got something and killed it.

Another time he said he was setting out 'maters clear out a piece past Squirrel Hollow. He and Monroe was sorting out 'mater plants, picking over 'em to get the trash out. There was an old car hood there. I think somebody throwed it over in the woods now. Monroe was right close to it, and he says, "Mr. C, I smells a snake in here somewhere. It's a copperhead." Clyde said he looked under the old car hood, and there it laid. I'll tell you one thing now: that old man had a nose.

❧

They always say if you kill a snake and hang it on the fence, it's gonna rain.

■

177

The Law & The Courts

"You want the sheriff, you call him."

People were better years ago. They were more honest. There wasn't all this stealing and robbing and dope like now. Nobody hardly locked their doors if they went away or to bed at night. You try that now and see what happens. You can have it all bolted and boarded up, and they still get in.

≈

It wasn't long ago, you could leave your gun outside. If somebody found it, they'd never touch it. Maybe they'd wrap it up so it wouldn't rust. That really happened. A man come back from ducking and left his gun in the boat. Somebody found it and wrapped it up and shoved it up under the front to keep it dry. He never did find out who done that.

≈

The game warden one time – I laughed till I cried over that. Old Draper – he's gone now – he had a bad stutter. He would come in the yard and start, "Ho-ho-ho-ho." It would take him ten minutes to tell you: "Hold the dog."

I would say, "It's O.K. John; I know what you want."

This one day him and Willie was rabbit hunting, and Willie didn't have no license. Murphy and myself was out birding, and we stopped by the ditch. When we got out, I said, "There's somebody hunting over there." It was Willie and John. Well, we hollered over to 'em, asked if they'd scared up any birds. They said they hadn't, so we kept on straight across the county road. That land was so poor in

178

there it didn't get over ankle briers, but we found a covey or two of birds.

We got near about to the road coming back, and I said, "There's the game warden." He stopped right in front of us. When we got over there, he said, "You seen anybody rabbit hunting?"

I said, "Yeah."

He said, "Who was it?"

I said, "I don't know." Course I knew 'em all the time. He said, "One, by God, I never could get nothing out of him but 'ho-ho-ho.' The other fellow didn't have no license."

What they done: they'd gone over the railroad and down that hill to the edge of the branch, and they didn't see the man's car when he pulled up there. Just as they got to the railroad, there he was. He could of laid his hand right on Willie with no license. I forget what they called Willie's old dog, but he was a good rabbit dog.

Willie said, "My Lord, he saved my hind. He jumped a rabbit just about the time that warden come down the bank. I started walking backwards saying, 'Look out, he's coming out here,' and pointing my gun." That old warden was standing back. He didn't want to get shot. Willie got out of reach, and he flew. It was a wild place in there, and Willie put hisself right in it.

John stayed there. He had his license. The man tried to get him to tell who it was, but all he got out of him was, "Ho-ho-ho." He didn't say nothing else.

And what Willie done: he run all the way around that branch, and he was standing in his door watching the man when he went by. He come down that night to tell me. There wasn't many wardens in that day. It's the only one we ever had that asked me about my license.

ᶻᵃ

They hated anybody was a game warden.

ᶻᵃ

I always heard the story that somebody caught a game warden by hisself one time and like to beat him to death with a goose. I heard that story ever since I was a little boy and never knew who done it. I was asking Captain Ben one time if he knew who it was. He said, "Yes I do. It was me."

I said, "Well, tell me about it."

He said he had geese baited, and a warden come on the Island. He put some bait out and went home to eat. When he got back, he said it was one goose in the creek, and he shot it. He stuffed the goose in a bucket he carried corn in and was walking back. He come around a corner, and the warden stepped out and said, "Hold it there fella. I'll take that goose."

Ben said, "You just as well better get ready for it then."

He said he dumped that goose out of that bucket and grabbed it by the neck, and when he got done beating him, that warden was crawling across the bridge, and there were nothing left but that goose's neck. He beat the body all to pieces. "Then I got scared," he said. "I was afraid he'd crawl off somewhere and die."

He crab potted till he was in his seventies. He was heading out one day, and a Coast Guard man jumped in his boat. He was already under way. He looked at him and said, "Young man, I'm gonna do you a favor. You see that little point of land over there? When I go by it," he said, "you better damn well jump for it." And that boy did. He almost got in a mess of trouble that time.

He hunted for the market and loved it. He had a gun would shoot ten shots. He had an extension tube. One of the best shoots he ever had: he said he shot eighty some ducks with one round of emptying the gun. There were some ducks in them days.

೭ಎ

Lem's on a round again. Buffy come by yesterday and

wanted me to call the sheriff. She got me in trouble: Two or three times I called the man for her, and she wouldn't have nothing done with him. She come in one day, man, she was bloody as a hog, and her dress was tore off her. "Call the sheriff come get Lem! He near about to kill me!"

I called him up here, and she wouldn't have a thing done with him. "I'll be danged if he kills you," I told her. "If I see you laying in the road, I'll never call him again. You want the sheriff, you call him." It ain't no use. She wouldn't do nothing with him. Then you have to call the sheriff for yourself, and he wouldn't want to come, and I don't blame him.

❧

Two women down here shot their men and killed 'em dead, and I don't blame neither. That one bastard – I'd give him a black pill a long time ago. He was a bad one.

❧

They had a bank robbery up to Hurlock today. This fella lives just a few doors from the bank. They got a good picture of him; they say so. Of course they all know him anyway. He come in there with a bag. Fellow right outside said he was carrying that bag in his hand, and when he come back out, he had it under his arm and was hurrying a little more.

Course I went up there right in the middle of it to get some seed. When I made the turn, I seen all these trooper cars by the bank and troopers walking all up and down the street. I pulled in beside the store in the parking lot there. This trooper car was setting with a hole by it, so I pulled my pickup right in there. He had the purtiest dog in that car, and he was vicious. He wanted to get a hold on me bad.

So I walked around by the porch, and there was Brooks.

"Just robbed the bank," he says.

181

"The devil they had," I said. "Well, they ought to turn that dog out. He wants to eat somebody up."

Brooks said he seen him when he went by. He spoke to him. Said he had this bag in his hand, and when he come back, he had it under his arm and was walking a little faster than before. He come from the bank and went right across to the store and down the alley. He went on home and pulled his clothes off that he had on to get the money. There laid his clothes in the house. Then he took off. I guess he knows where he wants to spend that money. They'll catch him. They know everything about him, and he didn't get enough to go far. He only went to one teller.

Betty come by there a little while ago and said the law was setting on the doorstep. I guess they're waiting for him to come home.

They used to have an alarm running from the bank across to the store. If something happened in there, they were supposed to call the law. For years and years nobody didn't break in, so they done away with it.

They done the same in Vienna. They run the wire from the bank to Hurst Hardware across the street. They took that out too, and they had a robbery right after they pulled it out.

·&·

I remember when they first built the bank in Vienna. Of course it burned down, and they had to build it over again. They made a big fuss about putting your money in there to keep it safe. A fella down in Kraft Neck said, "I ain't gonna put my money in there. They got meeces in there." Of course he meant mice. He told me: "Them meeces will eat it right up and make beds out of it. I got a place where I hides mine. I got a oak tree with a hollow into it, and I put my money in that hollow." I seen him later on, and he said, "I showed a man what a pretty place I had to hide my money, and I went the other day to get some to buy 'baccer for my pipe, and there wasn't none there." I guess he had meeces into his hollow too.

I remember when that bank burned down. My father came down the next morning and said the bank burned, so we went up there. They had a safe in there looked like a potbellied stove – three feet tall and steel. Some of the big shots were standing around, and they thought the money was gone for sure. Somebody was throwing water on the safe, and it were steaming. Finally they got it cooled down, and whoever knowed how to open it got it open. And the money was all right. What money was in there wasn't even scorched, and that bank had burned right down flat.

કન્

White and colored got along good in the old days. Daddy and Saul would go coon hunting together. They'd go to the colored church, tie their dogs outside, and go right in. The colored ones would keep two seats right there for 'em. They was always welcome.

Edgar would go down to that colored church too. He was down there the time they killed that fella right there in the churchyard. He was a bad one. He was wanted. He killed somebody.

The sheriff told him, "I'll give you five minutes to get as bad as you can get, then we'll see what goes on." He shot him right out the front of the church.

Old man Edgar said it was a time; said he couldn't get out the door for the rush. He said, "Damn a church with only one door." He went right out through the window.

કન્

Some guy killed this fellow in Church Creek one time, and he hid out in that marsh for months. He went out there to one of them islands off Blackwater Bridge. There used to be trapping shanties all over that marsh. They claim his mother would hide a meal for him under the bridge, and

183

that's how they caught him. Damn if I don't believe he hit that fellow on the head with a pop bottle.

ஃ

We've had some common sheriffs in the old times. A bushel of oysters and a dozen soft crabs could get you off murder at one time. Now you take the Fanny Neeman mess. I know you heard a sketch or two of that. Her sister said she went off to pick figs or something and never come back. They had hundreds of people out there looking for her, bloodhounds and everything. They never found a stitch. She lived with her brother and sister, and she was married to some old man who was married to her daughter one time. He run off from the daughter and married the mother.

It was forty years ago, I guess, but you still hear about it every now and then. They started it all up again some years ago. They got a letter or something from somebody. It was supposed to be new evidence. They went in there with a bulldozer and dug around. They found an old well and figured she was in the well. They found some animal bones in there, but they never found nothing of her.

She was killed, and other people know it too. And they know who done it. He was a big-timer, big family name, and he was tied up with a big-time politician. Everybody would know that name too if it were told. Somebody would bring somebody else oysters every week for a long time after that and didn't charge nothing for 'em. The fella who killed her is dead now. They're all dead, but nobody will still mention it. Old ties run deep down there. Those people will still get you. It's no different than the Mafia in the city, just a little more laid back. The poor folk's Mafia.

ஃ

Man come in a while back; he said he just come to talk. He said shopping cost money, but talk was cheap. I told him I didn't know about that. Sometimes you can talk so much it gets you in a mess. I knew a man one time who talked so much he got three months. He told so many lies the judge give him three months for talking lies.

And there was one fellow – of course he's dead now – the judge give some time for beating his woman. I think he give him six months.

Man said, "That's all right judge, I can stand on my head for six months."

Judge says, "O.K., take twelve then, and you can use the other six to get back on your feet."

&

Some fellow over here would steal anything. He never did work as I knowed, and he had all kind of time to prowl around everywhere. This time he stole some old woman's money. Well, the sheriff finally caught up with him and hauled him off to the judge. The judge says, "What you got to say for yourself?"

The man says, "Well judge, I'm just a poor man what believes in the Bible, and the Bible says the Lord helps him what helps hisself."

"Is that so?" the judge says. "I guess you know then that the Bible says the Lord loves him what gives to others too. Now I certainly want the Lord to love me, so I'm gonna give you two years."

&

When old Ted was judge, he was comical. He'd find you guilty, and you had to go to church so many times.

Every Tuesday night was court night. They had it in that little house next to the firehouse. People would be butt to butt in there and more looking in the windows. Every Bob and Mary would show up.

You know that house that sits crooked down there? That used to sit up here. There were two of 'em, just alike. They had trouble. One fellow was running the other one's wife, that's exactly what it was. I don't know how it got to Ted, but they say that part of his sentence was that Sam or Cornell – one – had to move his house. First thing I knew, the house was hooked onto and dragged down there.

ॐ

If you went in the court in them days, you were guilty. The county or the state never did lose a case as I know. One time the judge up here looked at this man come in and said, "LeRoy, what are you doing in here? Didn't I tell you the last time you were in here that I wasn't gonna put up with this no more? Thirty days in the county jail!" He never did ask him why he was in there.

The sheriff could go to that judge and get a warrant anytime. The judge would sign a handful of 'em, and the sheriff would put 'em in his pocket till he needed one.

ॐ

The judges were magistrates at first. After a while they did away with the Magistrate Court and put in the People's Court. Ted was judge there too. One day he told everybody to stand up and sing happy birthday to Judge Farnell, and they done it; prisoner too.

Scotty was another judge. One day the State's Attorney got down on his knees, and Scotty asked him what he was doing.

"I'm looking for your marbles," he says, "'cause you done lost 'em."

■

Moonshining

"Them was a happy bunch of hogs."

There was this old fella Nathan, and he could hardly get around. I don't know how long I kept him. I found an old shanty back in the woods, back in the swamp at the sawmill. The track in there was a good two foot deep. You could get in with a mule and a wagon, that's all. The man what run that mill says if I wanted to buy that shanty. I says, "Yeah." I gave him twenty-five dollars. It was all rough boards they sawed up at the mill. I went in there with my mule and wagon and moved it back of the ditch. Nathan and I fixed it up a little. It was 1934 or 1935.

I had roads through that woods where I cut holly with my mule and wagon. I'd put it up in boxes for Christmas and ship it to the city. It's all growed up in brier now, but it was only just patches of it then. A bunch would go back there and push some leaves aside and shoot crap, and Nathan and Neal would furnish 'em whiskey. At that time they got the bootleg down to Little Mill.

One day somebody called the law on 'em. Ed was back there, but he got away through Peters Swamp. Another fella got scared when he heard the law coming and run right into a tree and knocked hisself out. They got Nathan. I was out there and seen the deputy walking him out. Nathan had a flask of that bootleg in his overalls pocket, and the sheriff was walking alongside of him. When they got to where some weeds was growed up, Nathan took that pint and put it out and kept right on walking. After the sheriff left, I went out there and got it and busted it over a stump. They done that every Sunday. They'd go there and shoot crap and drink the bootleg.

❧

The first still I ever seen – well, it wasn't the whole thing. This fella from down south married Kenny's mother, and they had a lot with a little house on it down there close to old man Chester's. He had a old Ford roadster with a little trunk on the back, and he made a pickup out of it. It was tore up this time, and he walked over here to get a load of groceries. I said, "I'll carry you home. I want to see that still I hear you got over there."

"Well," he said, "I ain't got it hooked up right now, but I can show you a part of it."

So we walked around his field. We kept walking, and him looking up every tree. I said, "Damn, you got a still up a tree, I guess."

"I got it scattered around," he said. "There's the coil." He points up a old oak tree.

Well, he got that down, and we looked at it. I didn't see no more. He had it scattered all over the woods.

❧

There was plenty of money in bootlegging one time. Babe told lots of tales about it. He used to have plenty of money stuffed everywhere. He had it here and yonder and everywhere else. He had a bunch of money, and nobody ever got none of it from him.

They come after him a couple of times. One time he had barrels setting right in the front yard just full of mash, and him setting right on one of them barrels talking to the man. They'd talk and talk, and they didn't even look.

He said the way he sold his whiskey was to take it to Cambridge. He'd get a jug in each hand and walk right down the street. Said they wouldn't pay no mind that way. He said if you try to sneak it around, they'd get you.

They finally did get him down here to Little Chicone

Bridge, just over the creek, over there in the cripples. They had an eye on him all the time. Sent him off to college, he used to tell it. It was Connecticut or someplace–a federal place. He said it was the best place he ever was at. Said you go out there and watch 'em play ball; good food; nice and warm; the doctor checking on you to see your health was right– he had a bad heart anyway. Man, he said it was a nice place. Said if his wife hadn't got sick he might of just stayed there. After he come back, he's start right in again.

❧

Babe was down there to me, and I made him another still before he was out two weeks. I made all his stills. I made stills for people all over the county, many and many a one. They had 'em stuck everywhere. I started to say I made a thousand, but I guess that would be exaggerating. I know I made more than a hundred all during Prohibition. I made stills all the way up till it come back to buy whiskey legal. I made 'em nights. I'd sleep in the daytime and make stills all night long. Good Lord, I made some fancy ones with heat indicators on 'em and clean-outs and dials and everything else. I made some round, and I made some square. Most wanted 'em square. I had two blowtorches, one heating while I used the other one. I kept two going all night long. It was a boiler and a tube I made. The tube was in coils. You put your mash in the boiler and whatever you want to put in it. People used this, that, and the other into the mash to make different tastes. I didn't never put no mash in one; I just made the boilers and the coils. I used to buy the metal in Salisbury. It come in copper sheets like a tin roof. I used to buy four, five sheets at a time.

You had people with all different ideas about stills: Some wanted 'em cheap and some wanted 'em real fancy. Some had you take indicators off automobiles where the heat gauge, you know, took the temperature. I'd put that in there so you could tell the temperature of the boiler. And

189

I used to buy them big filler caps what come on boat engines. I used to put them on so a man could get his arm in there and clean her out, wipe her all out. Otherwise, all you could do was to flush her.

It's a wonder it hadn't killed people. Well, I guess it done some. I've had people bring in stills to fix, and be slump in the bottom. I've taken and dumped it – turned it out on the cement – and next morning there'd be a hole eat in the cement a foot across. The first time I ever done that – poured some on the floor – the next morning there was a great big place where it foamed up and a great big hole in the cement. I said, "Good Lord! I wouldn't want to drink something made out of this thing."

I started my work about nine o'clock when most other people went to bed. I'd go back in my garage and cover up everything, all the windows, you know. Then I'd start cutting up the metal and solder it together.

ے

There's two holes on my back place where they said Hooper had some of his stills in there. Old Hooper made a lot of whiskey; course they all of 'em made whiskey.

Hooper and Horse got caught one time. Well, they got Hooper, but Horse got away. He run all the way to Rhodesdale; then he walked back and give hisself up to the revenue man. He walked down here and throwed both his hands up and said, "I'm the one you're looking for." Hooper done some time on that one. He'd make his whiskey; then he'd go up to the church and preach.

ے

Wilmer kept a still going all the time. When I first bought my place, there was a whole bunch of agents back there walking that branch all up and down. I said, "What you all want in here?"

"We're looking for Wilmer's still," the man said.

I said, "Well, I ain't seen it."

When they found it, it was right there to old man Chester, right back of the old barn. They had to have water to moonshine, and old man Chester had a pump there to his barn, and that's where Wilmer's still was.

&#x20a

I'll never forget as long as I live: Leon, the old man's son, went up there that morning to milk his cow. I think the agents come on a Sunday and stayed all day and that night. The skeeters was bad, and them out there all night – God! The old man was laying there sleeping, and they went right down on him. He had a gallon setting by his bed. The old man was getting plenty of it, but he had nothing concerned with the still at all. They looked at that jug, but in the end they didn't bother him none. They was after Wilmer.

When Leon didn't come back from milking his cow, his wife told me: "I want you to go down and see what's with Leon."

I got there and seen Wilmer's truck. He had some cantaloupes on the back and four or five jugs. The old man was wanting to know what was going on.

Government man said, "We're busting up this still."

Old man said, "Yeah, where it at?" That tickled me.

Man said, "Right there." It wasn't a hundred yards from his house. He said, "Old man, we know you isn't involved, but we seen you come out and take a drink."

Old man said, "Yeah, I drink all I can get," and he gone back in and lay up on the cot, the jug setting right there.

They had Wilmer already when I got there. He said he never seen nothing like it either, but they knew it was his still. So they gathered Wilmer up and taken him over to Salisbury. They wanted to carry Leon bad, but I said he just went down to milk his cow. He had this one good cow down there. So they carried Wilmer, and we went down and made bond for him.

Then I carried him up to Baltimore for the hearing. Twelve o'clock come around, and the man didn't have no whiskey to show and no piece of the still. Somebody said, "Now what they gonna do?"

I said, "We gonna carry him back. They ain't proved he had nothing."

Judge said, "Where's the evidence?"

Man said, "We didn't bring it."

So Wilmer was a free man. That's the truth. They didn't have a drop of whiskey for evidence.

❧

Well, I heard they'd been over there and cut up Wilmer's still. I carried old man Murphy over after they toted Wilmer off to jail. I said, "Let's run over there and see Wilmer's still. Let's go have a look." So we went over, and old man Chester told us where it was. Wilmer strained that whiskey. He had a old, felt hat just like you wore on your head. They said that's what he strained it through. And there was the still laying out there, and the barrels was all beat up with a ax. I said, "Well, now we seen a still."

❧

There was one time somebody had a still right to the edge of Leon's field back there. Leon seen 'em when they dumped their mash in his hog pen. The hogs eat it, you know, and there wouldn't be no evidence. Well, them hogs got all drunken up on that mash. Them was a happy bunch of hogs it was.

❧

Keefer was a federal agent. He lived right up here, and his brother-in-law lived right back there in the old house behind him. Hell fire! His brother-in-law made whiskey in that old house all the time and sell it bootleg. He run the barber shop for years and years and sell it out of there every day. I guess old Keefer never got no haircut.

୬

I used to sell wood, saw wood and sell it. I was cutting over there where that ditch goes all the way through that woods. There was a little lot back in there. Old man Bell and little Johnny – he weren't over five feet tall – they lived there. They was comical.

They had a chimney run up through that shack. It had enough space around it that the fattest coon ever could crawl right in there. And when it rained, I never did see where it rained in. I don't know how in the world. They had steps going up a ladder to where they slept over top there. It's a wonder they hadn't froze to death. There was a path where George would crawl through the lint to his bed – it must of been a foot deep – and Johnny, he'd go to another one in there. They fit and fussed all the time; didn't get along at all.

They caught George bootlegging five or six times and locked him up every time. Old man Jim would give him away. Jim lived right down where the chicken houses is now. He wouldn't work nohow and just prowled the woods and every place.

George had a little old barn where I went by to cut my wood, and he had his still in that barn, just setting there.

You could always tell when George was making ready to run the still. He'd come over and get four or five pound of flour. He'd make a paste out of it and put it around his coil where it was leaking air.

Well, I was hauling, and I knew old George was back there. He had an old pistol, a .32 or something, and it all rusted. I was going right by the barn, and I knew he had that thing running.

"Goddamn!" I hear him yell. "Don't stop here!"

I went on back in the woods to get another load. I said, "When I come back, I'm gonna look at that thing."

193

So I'd come back and dumped my load, and I stopped the old mule and started over there.

"Goddamn! Don't come in here! I'll shoot you!" him yelling and wavering that old pistol.

I wasn't scared of George, but I was mighty particular if the man come up there and I be in it too. But I seen what he had: He had an old copper tubing; then he had a barrel; then there was some kind of little stove to heat a boiler. "Goddamn! You got no business in here anyway," I seen enough and went on.

It wasn't no time till old man Stokes found it and give him in again. He got six months or a year that time.

ఇ

They had a bunch over there to Little Mill one time. They had an upright setting in there. I believe them boys was from the city. It was a big job, barrel after barrel of mash in there. I remember old Billy used to talk about it; he seemed to know something of what was going on. I'll tell you one thing was going on: Old Billy could drink it.

ఇ

There used to be a place in Hurleys Neck, down next to the marsh where the big waterpond is. Outsiders came down there. None of us knowed 'em or done nothing for 'em. I only ever seen one or two of 'em, but there was eight or ten head. They come from up in Jersey someplace, and they was professionals. They had a steam boiler like you used in a mill, a big boiler. They didn't make no gallon jugs or cans. They used big, wooden, charcoal barrels, and they hauled it all away. The revenue men never did bother 'em as I know.

ఇ

Up that lane goes back in there, below where I used to live, a fella in there used to make whiskey. Fred and old

194

Ned heard him tell he was gonna "realize" one night. When you heard him talking about that – that was the word – you knew he was gonna run the stuff off.

So they went over and got to drink it right as he run it out. It was 110, 115 proof, and they both got drunk. Old Ned walked Fred home, and when they got over to his house, Fred says, "Goddamn Ned, you're drunk. I'll have to walk you home to make sure you get there." So they walked back across the field to Ned's.

They got over there after a while, and Ned says, "Goddamn Fred, you're drunk." So they walked back again. The biggest part of that whole night they walked back and forth across that field. There were some tales told down there.

ॐ

Alvin made whiskey and got caught, but it never cost him a cent. He served his time, and his wife kept all the money he made. When he come back, he took that money and bought the farm out there; paid cash for it. I know that to be a fact. It wasn't much money to buy a farm in those times, but it wasn't no cash money in those times either. He stepped up and peeled it right off.

ॐ

People would drink anything. There was an old man who lived back there in a little shanty. He'd come up here and get a bottle of alcohol and drink it – rubbing alcohol. And he used to dig up some kind of root or weed and boil it, and he'd make a tea out of it. He called it "wickey." It was some kind of little green thing he'd find in the woods. He went just about anywhere to find it.

ॐ

Years ago, when the inspector would come down from Baltimore checking on the bootleggers, they used to publish it in the paper so everybody could be wise and hide

195

everything. One man I knew used to hide it down in the ashes of his stove. Another one would put it under the horse feed, right down in the trough. If the man come, he'd throw something special in there. The old horse would be eating, and the man never even look. But old Calvin had the best place: He put it down the outhouse. One time, he used to tell, the man pissed right on the jug.

ઢ

There used to be two boats: the Hiawatha and the Whippoorwill. They'd come up the bay and have different stopping points. They were like PT boats, something like that, and they were fast. They carried a lot of liquor.

They finally caught one of 'em down in the lower part of the county, down in the Neck District. They caught 'em tied up in one of them creeks. It was a bit of shooting, I heard, but I don't think nobody got killed.

Everybody knew when the boat was somewhere close 'cause these big trucks would come down the road in the middle of the night. They'd come down loaded with produce and go back before daylight with liquor under the produce. People always said the Kennedys owned the boats, and that's how the old man made his money.

ઢ

The Whippoorwill used to come up here. One of the biggest places she would stop was Lewis Wharf. She didn't go no farther than Vienna. She would put off her stuff and turn around and go back out. She was a forty-five footer and had two engines into her, and she could fly. They didn't come till twelve or one o'clock in the night. Old Tommy was a whiskey man, and he was always waiting for her. He run the wharf at that time. I never did get involved with it. I never was much for getting drunk and falling down.

ઢ

One time during Christmas, a party give me a big old bottle of wine. I greatly appreciated it, but things like that can get you in a mess, you know. I don't drink it, and if I give it away, well now, it's just as wrong to give it to somebody as to drink it yourself. So I poured it out and kept the bottle. It's a pretty bottle.

■

*"She was a great institution,
the Model T."*

The roads were nothing but clay when I was a boy.
That was something with people driving in a Model T
and stuck all the time with them little, skinny tires. You
get behind her and push, and she'd cover you right up with
mud. It was an awful looking mess by the time you got home.

After about 1920 they got more oyster shell roads. They
were all right. You had to keep putting some on all the time
though. That old clay and mud ate them up.

The man who brought the mail up from Elliotts Island
every day had a time. After you got past Crossroads, it was
mostly pine poles laid all the way across them marshes.
Later on they covered over them poles with shells.

෨

I had a single-cylinder Excelsior. It was an Autocycle,
about a 1914 or '15, somewhere along there. She was a
right smart motorcycle. People all wanted to look at it.
She had one gear forward. If you got caught up in the
night, she had a headlight on her and a tank with acety-
lene gas. You'd get off and open your lid and turn the gas
on, take a match and light it off. It had a reflector on back
of it. You could turn it up like a coal oil light, brighter or
dimmer, and a taillight the same way. It had a hose went
to both lights from the tank. You didn't use 'em much
'cause it cost eighty-five cents to get that tank filled.

I took her to Elliotts Island once. It was a pole road
down there, pine poles put all across the road and oyster

Transportation

shells in the middle. I had a job getting down there and back.

≥•

The first Model T we had didn't have no starter. You'd get up to the front and crank it. I cranked her so many times; I'll guarantee I've cranked enough to carry her all the way to New York if it been in gear. And that brake lever didn't hold nothing. She'd run right at you when she started. She jammed me against the barn one day, but I clumb up on the sill, and that's the only thing that saved me. If you jacked the hind end up and put her in gear, she would start nine times out of ten the first time you pulled up that crank. But if you throwed her out of gear, man, you could crank your eyeballs out, and she wouldn't start. She was a great institution, the Model T.

≥•

Before there was a lot of cars around, Jim Gillette went over to Salisbury. He decided to buy hisself a car, and he done it. It was an L Car – the name of it. You cranked her from the side. Anyhow, he didn't know how to drive. The salesman who sold it to him said, "Mr. Gillette, somebody have to carry you home."

"No indeedy," he said. "Just get me out of Salisbury. You can jump off then, and I'll go on home."

So he done it. He got home, and he didn't know how to stop it. He had a shed there, like a carriage house, and he was gonna put it in there. He drove in there and took the back end right out; made a circle in the yard and rammed into the woodpile. That shorted her out.

≥•

Before they had the bridge, they had a ferry over the Nanticoke. You could go free unless it was somebody from out of the county or state, but the state stopped paying the ferryman at sundown, and he'd charge you a quarter or fifty cents then.

It was an old scow, and there was a cable run across the river to hold her in line so the tide wouldn't take her all over the river. This cable laid down there, and she'd pick it up as she went along. There were hooks on the side of the ferry, one front and one back, and they took hold of the line. He had a little old gasoline boat he'd strap there beside this scow to pull it across. It was a little old Palmer motor, and it would go "putch, putch, putch." It run sometimes. If it didn't run, he had a stick he'd pull it across with. Most of the time he'd pull it across with that stick.

When you'd get to the other side and go across that marsh, it would look like you were going down a creek. There was water all over it and high reeds on each side. They put shells down there, but that marsh would eat 'em right up.

My Uncle Sam wanted to come to Vienna for something one time, and he carried me along. I was just a little kid, maybe ten years old. We had an old horse and a buggy. We got down there to that first creek – they called it Bridge Creek. It had a bridge across it. We were going over there, and here was this old fellow, Clarence Dashields. He had been to Vienna and come back. There was a crack in the bridge boards, and his horse's hind leg went in there and couldn't get back out. The old horse fell, and he was trying to rear up. Uncle Sam jumped out of the buggy and run there, and him and Clarence held that horse's head down.

He said to me, "You go up to old man Farmer's and tell him you want to borrow an ax. Tell him there's a horse in this bridge."

I did that. I was scared to death about that old horse. He let me have the ax, and I carried it back. Clarence held the horse's head down, and Uncle Sam cut that oak board. He cut it and got that horse out, and it didn't break its leg. We got Clarence straightened out and went on.

There was a little shed on the river shore to drive your horse in if you didn't want to carry it across. You'd tie it there till you went over to Vienna, but you better be back before sundown so you wouldn't have to pay.

I remember we got right to Bridge Creek one Fourth of July, Mom and Pop and my brother and myself. We had a Model T then, and it drown out just as we got to the bridge. The tide was up. We had to get off our tails and push it up on that bridge, and that bridge was up high. That Model T had a timer on the front of the motor, something like a distributor only they called it a timer. If any water got in that, it was the end of it. We had to dry her out.

When you got to the other side, over in Vienna, you couldn't get through the sand. There wasn't no road; just sand.

It's a shame it ain't like that now and keep that gang away from Ocean City every weekend. I tell you one thing: old Gene never would get that bunch across there. The old fellow lived by hisself and run that ferry. Gene Moore was his name.

 za

Winnie Webster lived in that old house, the first one going up Indiantown. He owned a canning house, and he had a nice farm. He was kind of a big shot. He wanted to go to Salisbury one day, and he had a pair of horses to a carriage or surrey. They got scared on the ferry and run right overboard with the carriage and all, and dang if they didn't swim ashore. When the horses were flighty, they would usually unhook them from the buggy or carriage. There ain't much you can do once you're out there in the middle of the river and they go overboard.

za

There were a lot of log canoes around one time, and everybody used to use a paddle or a sail to move their canoe

201

around. Some even stuck a pine bush up there for a sail.

Captain Luther had a store down in Hurleys Neck, and he kept his canoe where the creek makes up in there. Well, he went to Baltimore and bought a gasoline engine to put in his canoe. It was just a little thing, painted red, and it was called a Red Eagle. It had a picture of an eagle on the side of it. I was a little boy about three feet high, and my daddy took me down there on a Sunday morning to see Uncle Luther and his engine. Everybody went down there. He had it sitting down in the log canoe. I had a-hold of my father, holding his little finger, and I looked at that engine. That fascinated me. I loved to have that thing so bad. I wanted to get ahold of that so bad I didn't know what to do. It was the first gas engine I ever seen. Nobody knew how to hook it up and get it to work. I don't know what ever happened to it. I've been fascinated with engines every since.

&

This railroad went to Ocean City one time. It come from up near Claiborne on Kent Island and crossed over the Choptank River just below the Dover Bridge. It was a wooden bridge across there, and another one went across the Nanticoke right at Vienna. They pulled all the old bridges up now. The one down here would crack and snap when you went across. It's a wonder it never fell in the river with the train on there.

Mom used to bring us over from Mardela to Vienna on the train. Vernon Dennison had a big dry goods store there in Vienna. He had everything in that store. People come from everywhere.

The last time I seen the train come down here, there must of been a hundred cars hung to that thing, and on that old track. It was going down to the electric plant with coal. The rails broke twice before they got to Vienna and back, and that was only four miles. A man come up here and said the track had curled up. I went and looked, and there to that crossing, that track was curled right up in the air. So I called down to the plant and said the track broke – setting right up – and they better look before they come back up. They come up here and sent over to Delaware, and a bunch come and cut a place out and welded another piece in there. When they come back up here, that thing jumped the track and set there on the dirt. It set there a week with the engine running. They claimed they couldn't get it started no more if they cut it off. It set there: "chug, a-chug, a-chug, a-chug, a-chug." They must of had a lot of fuel in it, or else it didn't take much to idle. They finally come down and put her back on the track and brought all them cars out. That was the end of it.

ॐ

Around the First World War you went everywhere by train. In 1916 and 1917 Pop worked in Wilmington in the shipyards. Ed Bradley and Pop and Russell – a bunch of 'em – boarded the train right in Mardela and went up there. Mr. Ed's wife was going up on a train to see him one time, and Mom let me go along with her.

We left from Mardela and went to Salisbury. You had to change in Salisbury. When you got to the Delaware line in them days, colored people had to get out if they was in your car. They had to go and get in a car by itself. It was all right for you to ride together in Maryland, but when you struck that Delaware line, they had a car there for just them.

When we got to Glasgow, the train stopped. There was a little child out there asleep on the railroad track with his head on the ties. The train didn't see him fast enough, and it was over him before it could stop. Everybody got out and went back there and looked. That child never woke up when the train ran over there. If it had just raised its head up, something under that train would have hit it. I never will forget that kid – two or three years old – laying there asleep on that railroad track. They woke him up, and he was just fine.

≈

It was mostly trains if you wanted to go somewhere before the thirties. Maybe it was the late twenties when we got the Red Star Bus Line to go through here. They made one trip a day to Salisbury, Ocean City, Baltimore, Wilmington. If you went to Baltimore, of course, you had to go across the bay on the ferry. They had a garage and everything in Hurlock where they worked on the buses, and they left out of there too.

≈

There was a tube they had in the department store years ago. It went from the clerk to the office upstairs. Almost every store had one. The clerk would put the money in there with the slip. When she'd pull a string hanging on there, it would shoot that money upstairs. They would make change and shoot it back to the clerk. Fellow the other day asked me if I remembered that. I said, "I sure do."

"Well," he said, "I think they should do the same thing on a larger scale. They could set one end of that tube at Sandy Point and the other end in Ocean City. They could have a big parking lot at Sandy Point, and all them city folk could drive down there and park their car. Everybody could get in that tube; make it so it would hold a hundred people at a time. You could pull a string and "whoosh," it shoots 'em straight to Ocean City. Then they wouldn't bother us, and they could probably get there in thirty minutes."

■

The Weather

"It's What they say: in dry weather
all signs fail."

The man said, "It sure is a pretty day overhead."

I said, "Yeah, but I guess there ain't too many going that way."

ཁ

My father was the greatest one about superstitions. If somebody was moony, he was moony. He was the worst I ever saw. The moon and the wind and the tide had to be a certain way or he wouldn't do nothing, but he was good about the weather. Every morning he'd look at daybreak. If the day breaked real high: "Gonna have a good day today." If it was a long time getting light: "Wind gonna blow a gale today," or something. And there's a lot of truth in it.

I used to be in the marsh in my younger days before day broke. Sometimes it got a red stripe to the east and would fly right across from one side to the other; the whole sky would just light right up. And I seen it again: it just kept creeping along and creeping along. Then it's cloudy, rainy, or stormy. But if it flies right across, that's the best day.

ཁ

I've seen daybreak so many times I can tell you exactly what the day's gonna be when I see the first crack of light. I can tell you whether it's gonna cloud up or whether it's gonna be clear, whether it's gonna be windy or ca'm. I can

205

look at the sky when the light first comes to the east; I can look up and tell you exactly what it's gonna be. When she opens up a crack and goes right over, you'll have a nice day. But if she gets up a little way and stands, you better get somewhere. You better get your hat and coat. It's a bad day, wintertime or summertime, either one. It's gonna do something: rain, snow, blow, freeze – something. You mark my words.

ð

I never paid no mind when they talked about squirrels and rabbits and bugs and all the actions they take – if it was predicted to be a hard winter. But you can tell by the cap on the corn – if it's thick or thin. If it's thick, it's a hard one coming.

ð

The worst snowstorm we ever had around here was in 1966. It snowed almost three feet one day and night. There were drifts over your head. Some people were snowed in for two weeks.

But mostly winters used to be harder years ago. It was colder, and you had more snow. When I was young, everybody had a sleigh and horses. You could hear the bells on them sleighs everywhere. I don't know where all our old bells got to. My brother and I would look for somebody to race. There wasn't no traffic. Them old automobiles wasn't no good in the snow, and you could race right out on the road. We had a little mare, and she was right. We'd take any-body on.

ð

Once we had a big snow on the eleventh of April. We were plowing and had the field about half plowed up. It got cold that afternoon, and the wind come northeast. It started snowing that afternoon and snowed all night long.

206

It was still snowing when I got up to milk the cows. But the sun come up nice and warm, and by the time it went down, the snow pretty well melted away. It was the eleventh of April. I never saw that no more.

≈

One time I set muskrat traps the first of January and never got back on the pond till the first of March. It come up a freeze that night and froze the pond solid, and the ice never got out till the first day of March. It's not as cold anymore as it used to be.

≈

April borrowed ten days from March and killed the old cow. You know that old cow was poor; hadn't eat all winter and was nothing but bones. You could hang your hat on her anywhere. They'd want to put her out as soon as they got grass, but April borrowed ten days from March to keep the grass down and kill the old cow. I heard that many a time, them borrowing days.

≈

I seen a great blue fireball one time, just as bright as it could be. Looked like it bounced down from this pine tree and skidded and jumped all around on the road, and then it just disappeared. A man said it was "ball lightning."

≈

When we lived in Indiantown, I was setting out on the porch one afternoon, and this storm blowed up. A bolt of lightning struck down out there in the field, right in the center of that forty acres, and it throwed up a great cloud of dust. I never seen that before or again.

≈

This old man was cultivating one time and a storm

come up. They said it was a bad bolt of lightning. That old man looked right up to the sky. "Goddamn!" he said, "Put out in that black gum over there. That'll hold you." They said the electric struck that black gum and busted her to pieces. They said that's the only time they ever saw that old man scared.

ૐ

There was a fellow standing on the porch one time at Applegarth's Store. They always used to congregate there. A thunderstorm come up, and it was a bad clap of thunder and a bolt of lightning. This fella said, "By God, hit her again." They said that lightning struck the chimney right then, and he turned just as white as a sheet.

ૐ

A bad thunderstorm come up one day when we lived down below Mardela. Pop had a little shed there for the horses and cows and stuff. He went out to that shed after that thunderstorm and picked up half a basket of fish that dropped out there. I don't know whether we ate 'em or not.

ૐ

I never seen fog so bad as that place over on the river. John said he plowed halfway across the river there one time before he knew where he was. The old mule just kept right on going.

ૐ

You see that ring around the moon last night? That was the widest ring I've ever seen. You see a ring around the moon, and there's some weather coming. You look inside that ring: If there ain't neither star in there, it's rain or snow the next day. A star in there, and you get the day off. We've had three rings straight, and one star in there every night. Still ain't had nothing. The old timers knew it. That's all they had to go by.

≥≈

Pop used to see sundogs, two of 'em sometimes. He'd say, "Day or two, come some rain." I never did catch on to them sundogs.

But a dog now – we always had an old dog around. He'd come out here and start wallering, roll over and roll back and forth. "We'll have rain in a day or two," Pop would say. And sure enough, sometimes the next day.

≥≈

Old folks used to say when a month comes in on a Sunday, don't look for no good weather.

≥≈

I swore there was a storm off here last night. The sun went right down into a storm. I said, "We're gonna get something sure." Then I dreamt about Paul all night. Mom always used to say that when you dream about the dead, it's gonna rain, and I dreamed about him all night long. I couldn't get him off my mind, and I never did hear any thunder, and it never did rain. It's what they say: in dry weather all signs fail.

■

Death & Burial

*"Them bulldozers might of scattered him
everywhere."*

I heard Mom say that a crowing hen – an old chicken
hen when it would crow like a rooster – that was bad luck.
She said when her father died – she was young then – she
said a hen crowed just that morning.

୬

I'll tell you one thing: you had to be tough in the old
days. Either you was tough or you didn't make it. Weren't
no miracle drugs. You was either tough or they nailed you
up in a box and put you out back.

୬

When I was a boy and you'd go to a funeral, and a man
been dead three or four days waiting for somebody out of
town to come, his mouth would be foaming, you know. My
mother's father was like that. He died in the summertime
in hot weather. They had him laid out in the parlor, the best
room, and that's where they had the funeral, right there.
They didn't embalm him or nothing, and they didn't have
no ice or no cold place to put him. The undertaker had to
wipe his mouth every two or three minutes whenever anybody would come to look at him. When they kept 'em up
two or three days, they would be getting kind of bad. I've
seen it many a time.

୬

People used to die, they just nailed 'em in a box and buried 'em wherever they could. They didn't have many regular graveyards or no vaults in them days. They just buried people on their own property or back in the woods someplace. You can't do it no more. You ain't supposed to anyway.

You ain't supposed to tear up no graveyard neither. They're pretty heavy on you now if you do that, but years ago they done it plenty. At Shiloh there used to be a store. They built that store right on top of a graveyard. The mailman that come through here had people buried there. He raised the devil, but they done it anyway; just laid the tombstones down and built right over it.

And where the canning house is, a right smart graveyard there. I think they were all colored. There were tombstones all out there. I don't know what they done – pushed it in the woods or what. They had bulldozers out there leveling it up, and the graveyard disappeared.

The old ones what lived all over the place in tenant houses and shacks – when one of them died, they just buried 'em where they could. They didn't have no money or nothing. They buried a lot across the ditch. I know they tore up many a grave in there when the electric people run that line through. Ain't but one tombstone left, and it's down in the branch. I think there's one vault. The rest they just put in a box.

I remember when one died in the house that's still standing over there. His neighbor come over and said the undertaker wouldn't bury him till he gets some money. They kept him up about a week or so then already. I said, "Well, I'll give some, but I can't pay the whole burying." The county or the state wouldn't pay nothing then. So we give a little something on it, and some other people give a little something too. And they sold a hog he had in the pen there, and they put him out. He's over the branch. That's where they put him anyway. I can't say where he's

211

at now. Them bulldozers the electric crowd sent in there might of scattered him everywhere. They just drove over the colored cemetery, but they didn't hit the white cemetery there in the woods.

Old Sam's buried out there too. The old house he was living in fell down one time, and he didn't have no place to stay. We built him a house over there in the woods on Wilmer's. There were mills all over the woods then with boards piled up. We got the lumber at one and hauled it with a truck. We'd go over there on Sundays, two or three of us, and work on it. Built a two-room house, shanty-like. He was tickled living there in that woods. We run a chimney up, and it was warm in there. Sam was old then, and you didn't get no Social Security and all that stuff in those days. The old people just had to depend on somebody to give 'em something. Nine out of ten didn't have nothing.

ૐ

When I was about twelve years old, they took up this grave over to Mardela. This man's wife had died. Somebody said he treated her like a dog, but I don't know nothing about that. She had been buried – I don't remember if it was a year or what. He hadn't put her in a vault, and he decided to have her took up. We went out there at dinner time – it wasn't very far from our school – and her hair had growed out through that coffin. I'll never forget that. I guess the dampness and no vault. They put a vault there and put her into it. That was 1915 maybe.

ૐ

There wasn't no funeral homes much in them days. They used to just go to the house and embalm 'em and set 'em up there. They stayed there till they buried 'em. I helped do one right over to Little Mill where that brick house is – Henry's wife. She was a little, teeny old thing. She died upstairs – double pneumonia. She was an elderly

212

woman too. Well, we brought her downstairs. It was a good thing she wasn't big. Them stairs wasn't very wide, and they turned every which-a-way. You had a parlor then. We put her in the parlor.

Howard Willoughby was the undertaker from East New Market. He went out to his car and brought in a stand and some jugs. This was on a Sunday night. He set the jugs on a stand, you know, to let this embalming fluid in. Well, he started to work on her, and the jug hung up above so it was gravity feed. The old man commences to cutting under her arm with razor blades – bleed her, you know. He says anybody dies of pneumonia it's a job to get that blood out. Everything closes up, he says. I don't know. Anyway, I hold her arm up or what he wanted me to do. I didn't know nothing about it. It was the first time I ever helped. Then he run that embalming fluid into her. I guess you had to get the blood out so that would run in there. There wasn't no force to it, just gravity. I don't think it would be a good job for me. Well, that time it was all right. It didn't bother me none.

&

Pick a rainy day to bury somebody, they say, and the spirit will go to heaven. The day we buried Mom: I don't think it ever rained no harder than it did that day. God! It poured.

GLOSSARY

black pill – poison.

cat squirrel – Delmarva fox squirrel, currently an endangered species.

cattybiasoned – at an angle.

colter – a sharp wheel attached to the beam of a plow to cut the ground in advance of the plowshare.

come here – one who is not a native.

cripples – swampy woodland bordering a river or stream.

gradiphone – Gramophone.

granner bag – a grain or burlap bag.

hanner – the common or "yellow shafted" flicker, a migrating woodpecker.

killdee – killdeer, a plover that usually lays its eggs on the bare ground of fields.

pine shats – pine needles.

sassprus – the sassafras tree.

shaves – shafts extending forward from each side of a cart to which a draft animal's harness is attached for pulling.

singletree – a center-pivoted crossbar attached to a wagon or farm implement and in turn attached to traces extending from a draft animal's harness.

snake frame – a shed skin.

the man – an officer of the law.

turkle – turtle, especially a snapping turtle.

tussock – a tuft or clump of grass.